DAVID NORTH

Freedom of Information Handbook

BLOOMSBURY

First published 1990
by Bloomsbury Publishing Limited, 2 Soho Square, London W1V 5DE

Publisher's Note
The information in this book was correct to the best of the Author's and
Publisher's belief at the time ot going to press. While no responsibility can be
accepted for errors and omissions, the Author and Publisher would welcome
corrections and suggestions for items to include in future editions of the book.

British Library Cataloguing in Publication Data

A CIP record for this book is available from the British Library

ISBN 0 7475 0570 5

10 9 8 7 6 5 4 3 2 1

Designed by Geoff Green
Typeset by Discript, London
Printed by Richard Clay Ltd, Bungay, Suffolk

Contents

INTRODUCTION

❝　The paramount function of this distinguished House is to safeguard civil liberties rather than to think that administrative con-
venience should take first place in law.

> Margaret Thatcher MP, House of Commons, February 1960

❝　Mrs Renée Short asked the Prime Minister whether she intends
to bring forward legislation to establish a public right of access
to official information.
The Prime Minister: 'No.'
Mrs Renée Short asked the Prime Minister if she is satisfied
with the current public right to access to official information.
The Prime Minister: 'Yes.'

> *Hansard* report of parliamentary questions, April 1987

The Prime Minister's mail is opened at about 9.00 am. A civil servant runs
through it quickly to see if there are any documents or correspondence that
should be kept secret. The rest goes into a folder which is available for public
inspection – anyone can go into the Prime Minister's office and demand to
see it.

However, this Prime Minister's office is not located at 10 Downing Street,
London SW1, but at the Riksdag building in Stockholm. In Sweden, every
citizen has a constitutional right to read official correspondence and documents under the Freedom of the Press Act. In Britain, there is no equivalent
freedom of information law.

In fact, Britain is the most secretive state in the so-called developed world.

- Officially, the British Telecom Tower in central London does not exist. It is an official secret because the 619-foot landmark does not appear on the official Ordnance Survey maps.
- How long is the queue at your local post office? The answer is an official secret. The Post Office regularly monitors how long customers have to wait to be served at its 1400 post offices, but we aren't allowed to find out the results. Post Office Counters Ltd claim this secrecy is necessary for 'commercial reasons'. Even the Post Office Users' National Council – the body representing the consumer – has been prevented from making the information public. If they were to tell the public or press, future information would be withheld by the Post Office.
- In July 1989, the Labour MP for Nottingham North, Graham Allen, tabled a parliamentary question asking the Prime Minister 'if there is an interconnecting door between Number 10 and Number 11 Downing Street'. The Prime Minister duly replied that there was just such a door. However, minutes after the reply was published, civil servants rushed around the House of Commons press gallery demanding that the Prime Minister's reply should not be used and that all copies of the reply be destroyed. Apparently the answer to Mr Allen's question is, in fact, a secret.
- Also secret is a British Rail report commissioned by Parliament entitled *Report on Track Pollution Problems 1957*, the result of our legislators' concern at the health hazards caused by thousands of tonnes of untreated sewage that each year are flushed from train toilets on to railway tracks up and down the country. Thirty-three years later, that unpublished report is kept locked in the office of BR's director of health and safety because the British Railways Board does not want to reveal its content to the public. It simply believes that the public has no right to that information.

The problem goes much deeper than that. The following is a list of 89 British laws which make the disclosure of information a criminal offence. And these are in addition to the infamous Official Secrets Act, 1911.

- Census Act, 1920, section 8(2)
- Coal Act, 1938, section 53
- Essential Commodity Reserves Act, 1938, section 1(3)
- Population (Statistics) Act, 1938, section (4)2
- War Damage Act, 1943, section 118
- Water Act, 1945, section 48

- Water (Scotland) Act, 1946, section 72(6)
- Atomic Energy Act, 1946, sections 11 and 13
- Coal Industry Nationalization Act, 1946, sections 56 and 57
- Agriculture Act, 1947, section 81
- Cotton (Centralized Buying) Act, 1947, section 23(2)
- Industrial Organization and Development Act, 1947, section 5
- Statistics of Trade Act, 1947, section 9
- Civil Defence Act, 1948, section 4(4)
- Cotton Spinning (Re-equipment Subsidy) Act, 1947, section 4
- Monopolies and Restrictive Practices (Inquiry and Control) Act, 1948, section 17
- Radioactive Substances Act, 1948, section 7
- Prevention of Damage by Pests Act, 1949, section 22(5)
- Food and Drugs Act, 1955, sections 5(3) and 100(5)
- Army Act, 1955, section 60
- Air Force Act, 1955, section 60
- Food and Drugs (Scotland) Act, 1956, sections 5 and 36
- Clean Air Act, 1956, section 26
- Naval Discipline Act, 1957, section 34
- Cinematograph Films Act, 1957, section 5
- Agricultural Marketing Act, 1958, section 47
- Offices Act, 1960, section 9
- Radioactive Substances Act, 1960, section 13(3)
- Flood Prevention (Scotland) Act, 1961, section 34
- Covent Garden Market Act, 1961, section 32
- Factories Act, 1961, section 154
- Public Health Act, 1961, section 68
- Rivers (Prevention of Pollution) Act, 1961, section 12
- Offices, Shops and Railway Premises Act, 1963, section 59
- Water Resources Act, 1963, section 112
- Weights and Measures Act, 1963, section 48
- Agriculture and Horticulture Act, 1964, section 13
- Harbours Act, 1964, section 46
- Industrial Training Act, 1964, section 6
- Cereals Marketing Act, 1965, section 17
- Gas Act, 1965, Schedule 6, paragraph 9
- Highlands and Islands Development (Scotland) Act, 1965, section 12
- Rivers (Prevention of Pollution) (Scotland) Act, 1965, section 11
- Abortion Act, 1967, section 2(1)

- Agriculture Act, 1967, sections 24 and 55
- Companies Act, 1967, section III
- Iron and Steel Act, 1967, section 43
- Legal Aid (Scotland) Act, 1967, sections 18(2) and 4
- Medicines Act, 1968, section 118
- Sewerage (Scotland) Act, 1968, section 50
- Trade Descriptions Act, 1968, section 28
- Post Office Act, 1969, section 65
- Transport (London) Act, 1969, section 36
- Agriculture Act, 1970, sections 21, 83 and 108
- Sea Fish Industry Act, 1970, sections 14(1) and 42
- Civil Aviation Act, 1971, section 36 as amended by the Civil Aviation Act, 1978, Schedule 1, paragraph 6(9)
- Fire Precautions Act, 1971, section 21
- Highways Act, 1971, section 67(4)
- Town and Country Planning Act, 1971, section 281(3)
- Legal Advice and Assistance Act, 1972, section 6(1)
- European Communities Act, 1972, section 11(2)
- Harbours (Loans) Act, 1972, section 2
- Town and Country Planning (Scotland) Act, 1972, section 266
- Employment Agencies Act, 1973, section 9
- Counter-Inflation Act, 1973, Schedule 4, paragraph 4 as amended by Price Commission Act, 1977, Schedule 2, paragraph 9
- Fair Trading Act, 1973, section 133
- Consumer Credit Act, 1974, section 174
- Merchant Shipping Act, 1974, section 14(8) as amended by the Merchant Shipping Act, 1979, section 40(1)(b)
- Slaughterhouses Act, 1974, section 20(4)
- Control of Pollution Act, 1974, section 94
- Legal Aid Act, 1974, section 22
- Rehabilitation of Offenders Act, 1974, section 9
- Health and Safety at Work, etc. Act, 1974, section 28
- Biological Standards Act, 1975, section 5
- Sex Discrimination Act, 1975, section 61(2)
- Supply Powers Act, 1975, sections 5 and 6
- Iron and Steel Act, 1975, section 33
- Industry Act, 1975, section 33
- Race Relations Act, 1976, section 52(2)
- Energy Act, 1976, section 18(2) and Schedule 2, paragraph 7
- Restrictive Trade Practices Act, 1976, section 41(3)

- Rent (Agriculture) Act, 1976, section 30
- Aircraft and Shipbuilding Industries Act, 1977, section 52
- Consumer Safety Act, 1978, section 4(3)
- Transport Act, 1978, section 11(2)
- Estate Agents Act, 1979, section 10
- Weights and Measures Act, 1979, section 12
- Agricultural Statistics Act, 1979, sections 3 and 4
- Banking Act, 1979, sections 19 and 20

This list was provided by a Minister of State at the Home Office in 1980 in response to a parliamentary question. A number of additional laws prohibiting the disclosure of information have since been added, and the total is now believed to be well over 100.

However, it does not need restrictive legislation to make something an official secret, as members of the National Council for Civil Liberties (NCCL) found when they conducted a survey of the 14 magistrates' courts in central London. They were aware that the public has the legal right to obtain from any magistrates' court a list of the names of the magistrates who sit there. However, all 14 courts refused to supply that information.

In Britain, secrecy is an obsession. But it is possible to conduct investigative research into the many organizations and individuals controlling our society – companies, government departments, the health service, charities, municipal authorities, Freemasons, lawyers – the list goes on and on. Researching that information is what the *Freedom of Information Handbook* attempts to help you do. In areas where the enquiring citizen will be carrying out primary research, such as investigating Companies House records or local government business, the information given in this book will be as thorough as possible. However, there are huge quantities of published information available on other categories – such as on the media and the various organizations that make up the political arena. In those cases, this book will be able to point you in the right direction, but it is not possible to list all sources of information here. So apologies are offered in advance for any oversights and omissions.

How, though, should people wishing to engage in investigative research go about it? The key is to remember that no individual or organization exists in a vacuum. If you want to carry out research on, say, building contracts awarded by a local council, you can make inquiries in a number of ways. These might include using business and trade directories; checking Companies House records; using the Local Government (Access to Information) Act; checking for a Masonic connection; and using press cuttings files. It is very difficult to provide detailed guidance on how to conduct investigative research, as cases will differ considerably – as will the amount of information available to the researcher.

However, here are a few tips that may help:

- Make regular use of the index to this book and learn to find your way around all the sections. Many issues overlap and interconnect, and not all of the information on any one issue will necessarily be in one place.

- For more detailed advice on research techniques and how to organize your research effectively, there is no better starting point than the excellent guide *Research for Writers* by Ann Hoffman, published by A & C Black.

- Don't take no for an answer. This suggestion is the advice of British Euro MPs Michael Hindley and Eddie Newman. When they wanted to find out what food was stored in their constituencies by the UK Intervention Agency – the custodians of our wine lakes and butter mountains – they were told that it was 'classified information for reasons of commercial confidence'. When they later posed as a meat trader and an ice-cream manufacturer and asked where they could obtain cheap supplies for the food processing industry, they were instantly supplied with the 'classified' lists. Therefore a little lateral thinking and the occasional act of subterfuge may be needed from time to time. Other examples are given in the book, but such skills develop naturally with the passage of time.

The British obsession with secrecy also means that everyone will at some time have cause for complaint against one secretive bureaucracy or another. Such grievances need to be pursued, and we all have guardians in our MPs, councillors and the press to help us fight for our rights. But in order to complain effectively, it is worthwhile consulting a small number of books which teach that skill effectively: *How to Complain* by Brigid Avison (Longman) is a good starting point. Des Wilson's two books on campaigning – *Pressure: an A–Z of campaigning in Britain* (Heinemann) and *Citizen Action* (Longman) – are also highly recommended.

Apart from encouraging the ordinary citizen to find and challenge secrecy wherever she or he finds it, the author and publisher of the *Freedom of Information Handbook* would like to receive feedback of your successes and failures, however small, for future editions. A limited amount of advice on investigative research is also available. But a reply – however brief – is only guaranteed if a stamped addressed envelope is supplied. Good luck with your investigations.

Where to go for further information

There are three main organizations that campaign about the issues of secrecy and freedom of information.

- Campaign for Freedom of Information, 3 Endsleigh St, London, WC1H 0DD, tel. (071) 278 9686. This is the key organization that campaigns against official secrecy and for reform of the secrecy laws. It publishes a quarterly newspaper, *Secrets*, available for an annual support subscription of £12.50.
- National Council for Civil Liberties (NCCL), 21 Tabard St, London, SE1 4LA, tel. (071) 403 3888. NCCL has been at the forefront of many campaigns against official secrecy, and publishes a number of books and briefings on the subject. A publications list and details of NCCL membership, plus information on its network of groups around the UK, are available from the above address.
- Community Rights Project, 5–11 Lavington St, London, SE1 0NZ, tel. (071) 928 5538. The project piloted the Local Government (Access to Information) Act, 1985 through Parliament, and campaigns for wider access to information and for greater accountability of local government. Details of the project's work are contained in Chapter 3.

Note: At the time of going to press, the telephone dialling codes for London were on the verge of change. Therefore, all the London telephone numbers in this book have been adjusted to reflect the new regime. Dialling codes for the rest of the UK remain as they were.

1 INVESTIGATING INDIVIDUALS

This chapter is divided into two parts: the first shows you how to find out what information is held on you by the State, companies, local government, official bodies, banks, credit reference agencies, the police – the list is almost endless. The second shows how one individual can research another – such as a company director, politician, civil servant, Freemason, professional person and a member of the social élite.

There is no law preventing one individual from investigating another without their knowledge or permission, so anyone doing just that should apply their own ethical code to their investigations. But it is the case that many decisions which affect our lives and the society in which we live are taken behind closed doors by people who may have obtained power through friendships, family ties and informal contacts. Often the reason for a political or business decision can only be established once information about the people involved in that decision has been pieced together. For example, what are the business interests of the councillors who passed a controversial planning application? Are any of them Freemasons? What other groups or organizations are they connected with? Who made the planning application? There are many sources of information that can be used to build up a profile of those with power.

What they know about you

But first, about you. Without a major Freedom of Information Act there is little opportunity for citizens to see the mass of information held on them by the many organizations we have to deal with during our lifetimes – government departments and agencies, financial organizations, local councils, schools, employers, insurance companies. In 1987, MORI polled 1909 British citizens, asking them, 'which of these records, if any, do you think you should have the right to see?' Their answers were:

- Your personal record held by your GP   73%
- Your own children's school records   67%
- Any records kept on you by banks, building societies and other financial institutions   64%
- Your personnel records kept by your employer   57%
- Your National Insurance/Social Security records   55%
- Government records to do with you, not having anything to do with national security   54%
- Government records to do with you, involving national security 36%
- None of these   4%
- Don't know/no opinion   6%

In fact, there are only four categories of information about you which you are entitled to see:

- credit reference files
- some local authority housing and social work files
- some medical reports
- information held on computers

Credit reference files

Under the Consumer Credit Act, 1974, every consumer is entitled to see any credit reference file that is held on them. A customer might, for example, make an application for a hire/purchase agreement but be turned down because he or she is considered a credit risk. But if the credit application does not exceed £15,000, the shop must provide the name and address of any credit reference agency used within seven days of being asked, or face a £1000 fine. The customer can then write to the agency, enclosing a £1.00 fee, and request a copy of their file. This, or a letter saying there is no file, must be supplied within 28 days. Credit reference agencies keep records on just about every household in the country. The two largest ones in the UK are CCN Systems in Nottingham and the massive Infolink credit reference system in Croydon. But beware. It has been said that anyone exercising their rights under the Consumer Credit Act will actually be marked as a risk, and may find it difficult to obtain credit in the future.

CCN Systems is at Talbot House, Talbot St, Nottingham NG1 5HF, tel. (0602) 410888, and Infolink is at Coombe Cross, 2-4 South End, Croydon, Surrey CRO 1DL, tel. (081) 686 7777.

CREDIT REFERENCE CHECKLIST
You have the right to:

- know if a credit reference agency has been used.
- be told the agency's name and address.
- obtain a copy of the credit reference file, or a letter saying there is no file.
- correct any inaccuracies that might be on the file.
- to ask the Office of Fair Trading to investigate any complaints.

Local authority housing and social services files

66 Public sector tenants sometimes believe that their landlord's files contain misleading personal information. In this area, and subject to proper safeguards, they ought to be able to check that mistakes are not being made.

Sir George Younger, Parliamentary Under Secretary of State for the Environment

Under the Access to Personal Files Act, 1987, individuals can inspect at least some of the local authority housing and social services files held on them. This right of access applies to social work clients, council tenants and people who have bought or applied to buy their council homes. They can inspect and make copies of their own files; have mistakes corrected; and put a statement of their own on file about any disputed matter. However, information that the powers-that-be think might cause 'serious harm' to applicants can be withheld – as can any information that may affect the privacy of others.

This right to access only applies to information recorded from April 1989, and councils can charge you up to £10.00 to see your file. The Campaign for Freedom of Information believes that this relatively high fee may deter many people from exercising their rights under this new Act.

HOUSING AND SOCIAL SERVICES FILES CHECKLIST
You have the right to:

- inspect some of the files held on you by social services
- inspect council housing files
- inspect housing files if you are buying your house from the council
- correct any mistakes that are on the file
- put a statement on the file about any disputed matter

Some medical reports

" One of the fears some doctors have is that people will read their notes and jump out of the window and kill themselves because they're so terrified. It's absolutely the opposite of what happens. In reality, it's tremendously reassuring to the vast majority of people. Even if they have bad news of a serious diagnosis, they still find it reassuring to know that they will have nothing kept from them. And if they don't want to know, they don't have to look in their notes. It is up to them.

Dr Brian Fisher, a London GP whose patients have access to their own notes

None of us has the right to read any medical records kept on us by our family doctors or at a hospital, although some GPs as a matter of principle do give their patients access to their records. One 26 year-old woman was astonished and appalled when her new GP accused her of being a heroin addict. It took her months to discover that an addict had been impersonating her at the health centre where her previous GP was based. And she only managed to persuade her new doctor to erase the references to 'addiction' by showing him her passport, which proved that she had been out of the country at the time when entries had been made on her notes.

'We consider that, as a matter of principle, patients should have the right to know what has been recorded about them [on their health records],' said Edwina Currie, the former health minister, in 1988. In May 1987, she inspected a new health computer while on a visit to the Derbyshire Family Practitioner Committee. To test the machine, Mrs Currie keyed in her own NHS number. The £70,000 computer was quick to demonstrate its abilities: it told her that she didn't exist. It was later discovered that the minister had been the victim of the type of common error that makes it so important for people to be able to check their own records – a clerical error had led to the wrong number being entered against her name.

However, the Access to Medical Reports Act, 1988, which took effect from 1 January 1989, does give everyone the right to receive a copy of any medical report supplied by their doctor to life assurance companies and employers. Patients then have the right to correct inaccurate information, and the right to prevent such reports from being forwarded if they are in any way unacceptable.

MEDICAL REPORTS CHECKLIST
You have the right to:

- inspect any medical report prepared for your employer
- inspect any medical report your doctor prepares for a life assurance company
- insist that any errors be corrected
- refuse to let the report be sent out
- complain to the General Medical Council if the doctor fails to cooperate

Data Protection Act, 1984

This is a complex piece of legislation (*see* Appendix 4 for an extract) that allows individuals to inspect the mass of data held about them on computers. For a fee, which can be as much as £10.00 for each inspection, copies of computer records must be supplied by the 'data user' once the 'data subject' has provided proof of identity. It is not possible, under the Act, to see anyone else's files.

DATA PROTECTION CHECKLIST 1
You have the right to:

- find out if an organization holds computer records on you
- know exactly what type of information it is
- inspect most of the computer files (for a fee)
- have any mistakes corrected
- have any complaints investigated by the Data Protection Registrar
- obtain compensation for the effects of any errors.

You do *not* have the right to inspect certain computer information, including information:

- used to safeguard national security

- used for crime prevention or catching offenders
- used for the assessment and collection of tax
- that may be sensitive, such as certain social services files
- on anyone else – you can only see files about yourself

The *Data Protection Register* (*DPR*), which is freely available for inspection at main reference libraries, is a fascinating document to look through. For example, as Barbara Cartland and Jeffrey Archer both use computers for their work, they have to register detailed information in the *DPR*, including their address and the type of work and the use to which their computers are put. It is only necessary for computer users to register under the Data Protection Act if they store personal details of individuals other than the users on computer. The entry for the police forces in the *DPR* is also very revealing. There is considerable criticism about the Act. A survey conducted by the Campaign for Freedom of Information to mark the Act's first anniversary revealed that many people were deterred from applying to see their computer records because of the fee; because of the lengthy and complicated application forms that have to be completed; and because many institutions fail to adhere to the Act's 40-day limit for responding to requests: 55 days after filing a request for information with the Police National Computer the Campaign had still received no reply. And in October 1988, the journalist Duncan Campbell reported in *New Statesman and Society* that, by using the Data Protection Act, it had taken him four months and a stack of £10.00 notes to find out nothing he had not known already.*

However, if you want to find out what information is held on computers about you, there are a number of useful guides on the Data Protection Act. The National Council for Civil Liberties has produced the 'civil liberty briefing' *Your Right to See Your File*, which is available from them for £1.00, as well as a more thorough booklet entitled *Data Protection: Putting the Record Straight*, by Roger Cornwell and Marie Staunton. The latter is written in plain English and explains this complicated law in a way that the layperson will understand.

DATA PROTECTION CHECKLIST 2
To find out what is held on you, the following steps need to be taken:

- Find out which library near you stocks the *Data Protection Register*. The Registrar's inquiry service on (0625) 535777 can help you.

---

* Addresses of most of the companies, organizations, agencies, etc. mentioned in this book are given in Appendix 1.

- Look up the company or organization in the Register's index.
- If they are registered as computer users, look up their entry in the main Register.
- Check the entry and make a note of the computer's registration number. Once you have this information, you need to contact the computer user and ask to see a copy of your entry.
- Write to them, quoting the computer's registration number, and ask to see your entry.
- Fill in any forms they might send you – they have to make sure that your application is genuine.
- Send the fee they ask for, which can be as much as £10.00 for each computer.

Other guides on various aspects of the Act are published by the Data Protection Registrar, the person responsible for enforcing it and handling complaints about any breaches. These should be available in any reference library, or else they can be obtained free from the Data Protection Registrar.

Investigating individuals

Many sources of information exist on individuals, and the more powerful the individual the more information will be available. Just consider the amount of press coverage and other published material on the Royal Family or Prime Minister. The golden rule is: make sure that any single source of information is double checked. For example, if your primary source is an entry in the telephone directory, ensure that you have the right man or woman by checking the address on the electoral register. The permutations of information are endless, and only some of the principal sources are listed here. The sorts of details that might be included in a personality profile built up during the course of an investigation are:

- Date and place of birth.
- Brief family history and spouse's background.
- Schools, colleges or university attended.
- Military service.
- Business directorships and shareholdings.
- Employment and income bracket.
- Past and present addresses and property details.
- Hobbies, informal networks and regular meeting places.
- If a member of one of the professions, who are the clients?
- Membership of a political party, positions held.

- Club and Masonic memberships.
- Public appointments.
- If a councillor, which committees and sub-committees.
- Criminal convictions.

And so on. This list is only for general guidance, and these suggestions would only apply to a major investigation, but it gives an indication of what information can be collated. Below are the main sources, but you should also use the index to this handbook thoroughly:

Telephone directories If you know the area in which the subject lives, then the local phone book is the place to start, although a subscriber can, of course, be ex-directory. Some libraries stock the entire range of directories for the UK; they now appear on microfiche. Back copies of all UK telephone directories since 1900 are available for consultation at the British Telecom Museum, 135 Queen Victoria St, London EC4V 4AT, tel. (071) 248 7444: public access Monday to Friday, 9.30–12.30 and 2.00–4.00, but it is best to phone first to make an appointment. Those from 1940 onwards are available for inspection at the City of London's Guildhall Library, Aldermanbury, London EC2P 2EJ, tel. (071) 606 3030.

Local directories The Thomson Local Directory is also worth consulting. Although it only lists commercial organizations in its main section, it also contains a directory of postcodes of large users – including all PO box numbers – and a street-by-street guide of postcodes. Always cross-check with the postcode directory as it may produce some useful leads. And the Post Office has confirmed that post office box numbers are not confidential; anyone can obtain the name and address of the subscriber by simply asking at the appropriate post office.

Town directories Find out from the local reference library if the town or city has a directory or year book. Some, such as Birmingham and Liverpool, have extremely comprehensive local directories that list all prominent dignitaries. However, many towns and cities do not.

Electoral registers Every occupier of premises in the United Kingdom is under a duty to register with the local electoral registration officer. That also applies to people who live on commercial premises, such as stewards of clubs who live 'above the shop'. The electoral register is available for inspection at libraries and council offices. The British Library's Official Publications

Library in London stocks a complete set of UK electoral registers. The Poll Tax Register (or Community Charge Register as it is sometimes known) is not available for public inspection, except that individuals are entitled to inspect their own entries.

Motor vehicle registration   It is not normally possible for a member of the public to obtain the name and address of the keeper of a motor vehicle from the Driver and Vehicle Licensing Centre at Swansea (DVLC). But if 'reasonable cause' can be shown for that information to be given, such as a minor accident or an infringement of private parking rights, then the DVLC might oblige. A request should be sent with a £2.00 fee to the Driver and Vehicle Licensing Centre.

Births, deaths and marriages   Since 1837, it has been a legal requirement for every birth, death and marriage to be registered. This information is held by the Superintendent Registrar of Births, Deaths and Marriages (check phone book) in each area in which they occurred, and certificates are obtainable by anyone for £5.00. The information is also held centrally at the General Register Office in London where the indexes are open to free public inspection. Copies of the certificates are available to anyone in person on the payment of a £5.00 fee. A postal search costs £11.00 if exact references are supplied, such as full names, precise date and locality; or £13.00 where reference information from the index is not supplied. Postal searches should be addressed to OPCS General Register Office, Postal Application Section, Smedley Hydro, Merseyside PR8 2HH.

Bankruptcy   A register of bankruptcy petitions and receiving orders (i.e. when a company has gone into receivership) is available for public inspection at the Thomas More Building, Royal Courts of Justice, Strand, London WC2. A postal search of the alphabetical index can be made by writing to the Superintendent, Land Charges Dept, Burrington Way, Plymouth, Devon.

Change of name   Anyone is entitled to change their name, as long as it is not for the purpose of deception or fraud, and there is no legal requirement for the name change to be formalized. However, if it is done by Deed Poll (e.g. when written proof of identity is required), the change may be registered at Room 81, Royal Courts of Justice, Strand, London WC2. Any Deed Poll registered more than three years ago will have been relegated to the Public Records Office.

Divorce   Copies of a *decree nisi* or *decree absolute* are available to anyone. These state the names of the parties, to whom the decree was granted, the grounds for the divorce and the date. Personal applications should be made to Room A44, Family Division, Principal Registry, Somerset House, Strand, London WC2R 1LP, tel. (071) 405 7641.

Wills and probate   Anyone can obtain copies of wills that have been lodged when probate or letters of administration were taken out. Generally that means wills that have been settled. An index of these can be inspected at Somerset House and then a copy can be obtained; postal applications can also be made. Grants of probate and letters of administration can also be inspected at Somerset House; these detail the name and address of the deceased and their personal representative, and the value of the estate.

Who's Who   This great tome contains biographical details of thousands of the UK's most prominent citizens – with a few exceptions. *Who's Who* should be one of the first reference books consulted in an investigation into individuals as many local and seemingly minor dignitaries often appear. Details include family background and relationships, education, service history, work history, company directorships, public service, publications, hobbies, club, and address. There are also some 44 subsidiary *Who's Who* titles, such as *Who's Who in Housing Finance* and *Who's Who in Britain's Railway Industry*.

Nobility   *Debrett's Peerage and Baronetage* is the complete guide to matters aristocratic, including a who's who of all titled UK citizens and royalty. *Debrett's* includes detailed information on hereditary lords and ladies, life peers, life peeresses, law lords, lords spiritual, the baronetage, the Royal Family, hereditary peeresses and peers who are minors, their clubs, a table of general precedence, forms of address of persons with titles, and so on.

Members of Parliament   All are listed in *Who's Who*. Further information is given in detail in Chapter 8.

Councillors   These are usually more obscure than MPs, but the local library should be able to supply a number of sources of local information on councillors, as should the council itself. Chapter 3 covers the detailed information that is available on local authorities and their members.

INVESTIGATING COUNCILLORS CHECKLIST
Information on councillors can be found in:

- the local council's publications
- old election literature in the local library
- local newspaper cuttings
- the town or city directory (if there is one)
- *Who's Who*, for prominent local dignitaries
- *The Municipal Yearbook*

Company Directors   A considerable amount of information on company directors is available to the public, and this is dealt with thoroughly in Chapter 2.

COMPANY DIRECTORS CHECKLIST
There are a number of ways of finding out who the directors of a company are:

- Ask at the registered office of the company – they are required by law to tell you.
- Check the *Directory of Directors*.
- Inspect the company's annual report.
- Check the detailed Extel cards.
- Obtain a copy of the Companies House files.

See Chapter 2 for further information.

People as companies   Some people engaged in profitable or controversial activities set themselves up as limited companies in order to benefit from limited liability and certain tax concessions. Examples of this are the Conservative MP Rupert Allason (pen name Nigel West) who trades as Westintel Research Ltd, and another writer on the secret services, Chapman Pincher, who operates as the company Summerpage Ltd. This practice is wholly legitimate, and such companies can be investigated in the same way as any other (*see* Chapter 2).

Property owners and developers   Although there is currently no fundamental right of access to information on the ownership of property, it is possible to piece together information from local government records and registers. This is covered in detail in Chapter 3.

Various Professions   A wide range of directories is published each year listing members of professional bodies, and *Current British Directories* lists most of them. Below are some of the key directories; and others are listed elsewhere in this book.

- ACCOUNTANCY: *Who's Who in Accountancy; Institute of Chartered Accountants List of Members; Institute of Internal Auditors Handbook; Chartered Institute of Management Accountants List of Members; Chartered Institute of Public Finance List of Members; Institute of Taxation Handbook; Association of Consulting Actuaries List of Members.*
- ARCHITECTURE: *Register of Architects; Royal Institute of British Architects List of Members; Royal Institute of British Architects London Region Year Book.*
- DENTISTRY: *Dentists Register; NHS Lists of Practitioners.*
- ESTATE AGENCY: *Incorporated Society of Valuers List of Members; National Association of Estate Agents List of Members; Royal Institute of Chartered Surveyors Yearbook.*
- FOXHUNTING: *Baily's Hunting Directory.*
- MEDICAL AND PHARMACEUTICAL PRACTICE: *Medical Register; Medical Directory; NHS Lists of Practitioners; Annual Register of Pharmaceutical Chemists.*
- VETERINARY SURGERY: *Royal College of Veterinary Surgeons Register; Veterinary Register of Ireland.*

Missing persons   The techniques used to trace a missing person will depend on how and why that person is missing. There are two ways of starting a trace. First, the Salvation Army can help trace a person's whereabouts, but due to the enormous volume of inquires they receive, this service is limited to near relatives for the purpose of reconciliation. The other source of advice and information is the book *Tracing Missing Persons* – an introduction to agencies, methods and sources in England and Wales by Colin D. Rogers. Published by Manchester University Press, this handbook is the most thorough guide to sources of information on an individual. Highly recommended, but reading it is enough to make anyone paranoid.

Tracing family history   Conducting extremely detailed research into an individual's background calls for the skills of tracing family history, or genealogy. This is covered thoroughly in *Trace Your Family History* by L.G. Pine. Published by Hodder and Stoughton in the 'Teach Yourself' series, this cheap and cheerful paperback is a gold mine of information on the subject, including: parish registers; local records; land records; archives; wills; records at the Public Record Office; useful addresses; sample family trees.

Newspapers The press is one of the most useful sources of information on any individual with even the slightest prominence. Reference libraries tend to keep cuttings about people in their area who have been in the news, and national newspapers and magazines are widely documented in press indexes. The subject of using press coverage as an aid to investigative research is covered in Chapter 7.

Further information

Apart from the various books referred to in this chapter, there are two other published sources that list the depositories of records and registers on individuals. *The Directory of Registers and Records* by Trevor M. Aldridge, although published in 1984 (by Oyez Longman), is still a very valuable and highly readable guide to statutory and official depositories of material. The other is *British Archives* – a guide to archive resources in the United Kingdom (published by Macmillan), which lists the over 700 libraries, institutions and record offices throughout the UK that keep public records and the like.

2 INVESTIGATING COMMERCIAL ORGANIZATIONS

With more than 1.8 million companies registered in the UK, many areas of our everyday lives are dominated by commercial organizations – not least because some are our employers, landlords and suppliers of public utility services. However, it is not only business organizations that are registered as companies; many non-profit organizations are registered as limited companies in order to benefit from limited liability, which protects their directors from personal bankruptcy and the effects of legal proceedings.

For example, public schools such as Winchester College and Cheltenham Ladies College are registered as limited companies, as are almost all the colleges that make up Oxford University. Other institutions of the British Establishment that are registered in this way include: All England Lawn Tennis Club (Wimbledon) Ltd; Carlton Club Ltd; St Bartholomew's Hospital (Nominees) Ltd; National Theatre Board Ltd; The Church Estates Development and Improvement Ltd; The Law Society Ltd; Royal Masonic Benevolent Institution (Services) Ltd; Lloyds of London Ltd; Frère Cholmeley Ltd (the Queen's solicitors). And even pit workers can glory in their membership of the National Union of Mineworkers Ltd.

Charities, partnerships, campaigning associations, professional bodies and voluntary groups are among the many organizations that are registered as companies – and this allows the public the right to obtain detailed information on their activities. Any thorough investigation of any type of organization – except, perhaps, small informal groups – should involve some use of business information sources. The amount of research carried out will of course reflect the amount of time and expense that particular research project warrants. (*See also* the introduction to Chapter 5 – Investigating the voluntary sector.)

COMPANY FINANCIAL INFORMATION CHECKLIST

Accounts and other financial information on a company will be found in:

- business directories such as *Kelly's* or *Kompass*
- the International Stock Exchange Official Yearbook
- Extel cards
- the company's annual report
- Companies House files

Company information

Under the Companies Act, 1981 and the Business Names Act, 1985, anyone carrying out business, whether an individual, a partnership or a company, must make certain information public when the business is carried out under a name *other* than that of the owner or owners.

- The name of the owner or owners must be shown on all:
  - business letters
  - written orders for the supply of goods or services
  - invoices and receipts issued in the course of business
  - written demands for payments of debts arising in the course of business
- The name(s) of the owner(s) of a company must be displayed prominently on any premises where its business is carried out. If the owner is a company, the name, Companies House registration number and address of the registered office must be displayed too.
- The names and addresses required to be disclosed must also be given immediately in writing to any customers or suppliers, if requested.
- Further details – including a number of other detailed requirements that apply to the use of business names – are contained in a Department of Trade and Industry (DTI) leaflet *Notes for Guidance on Business Names and Business Ownership*. This is available without charge from the Chief Executive and Registrar of Companies, Companies House, Crown Way, Cardiff CF4 3UZ, tel. (0222) 380362.

Companies House

Every company is required by law to make an annual return to the DTI at Companies House, providing the following information:

- Address of registered office.
- Summary of share capital issued.
- List of past and present shareholders, showing names, addresses, numbers of shares held and transferred since the last annual return.
- Particulars of directors and company secretary, including addresses, nationalities, business occupations, dates of birth and details of any directorships held. Details of changes of directors must be filed with Companies House within 14 days.
- Amount of indebtedness in the form of mortgages and other charges.
- Summary of debentures.
- A copy of any balance sheet put before a general meeting.
- A certified copy of the auditor's report.

All of this information is, for a fee, available to the public in the form of a microfiche from Companies House. This may be a worthwhile investment if detailed research of a company is required (but see also Extel, p. 21). The Companies House microfiche can be obtained in three ways:

- BY VISITING COMPANIES HOUSE: A visit to one of the Companies House offices may be convenient for some people. There are offices in London and Cardiff where documents on companies registered in England and Wales can be obtained, and ones in Edinburgh and Belfast for companies registered in Scotland and Northern Ireland; see Appendix 1 for details. The fee for one company's microfiche is £2.50.
- POSTAL SEARCHES: For many people it will be necessary to pay for a postal search, and this costs £4.50 for each company. For most companies, the file will include a list of their shareholders, but if it is a large public company, such as British Gas or British Telecom, there is an extra charge for long shareholders lists.

  The request for a microfiche must include the full name of the company, the Companies House registration number of the company (this information, together with other key information from the Companies House index, is available without charge from Searchline, a service provided by a commercial search company, ICC Company Information Services Ltd, on (071) 251 4941), and a cheque or money order made payable to the Registrar of Companies. This should be sent to the Companies House in Cardiff (for companies registered in England and Wales), Edinburgh (for Scottish Companies) or Belfast (for Northern Ireland). The envelope should be prominently marked 'Postal Search Section'. The documents will normally be sent out within three working days. Further information and advice about postal searches is available from Companies House at Cardiff on (0222) 380107/380108.

- AGENCIES: A number of commercial agencies will be able to obtain Companies House documents on your behalf, but a search of this type will cost around £23.00 for each company. The main agencies are: ICC, 16-26 Banner St, London EC1Y 8QE, tel. (071) 251 4941; and Jordans, Jordan House, Brunswick Place, London N1 6EE, tel. (071) 253 3030. However, some public libraries can obtain Companies House files at the £2.50 cost price, so check with your main reference library first.

COMPANIES HOUSE CHECKLIST

The files at Companies House will reveal a wide range of information, including:

- names of all directors
- names of the company secretary
- shareholders
- types of business carried out
- copies of accounts and balance sheets
- company history

Registered offices

Under various sections of the Companies Act 1985, the public has the right to obtain access to certain documents at the registered office of a company, usually upon payment of a nominal fee of 5p for each piece of information.

- Under Section 356, a register of members (shareholders).
- Under Section 288, a register of directors and company secretaries, including their full names, residential addresses, nationalities, business occupations and other directorships.
- Under Section 219, a register of directors' interest in shares (no fee required).

- Under Section 407, a register of mortgages and other charges.
- Under Section 191, a register of debenture holders.

Therefore, if the company has a local registered office, it may not be necessary to obtain the Companies House file. An inquiry should start with a letter to the company secretary at the registered office asking for an appointment to inspect the registers. If that fails, visit the office in person anyway and be persistent. Expect a cool reception.

A criminal offence is committed if any company fails to comply with its legal duty, either in making registers available for inspection at the registered office, or in filing documents at Companies House. The matter can be reported to the Companies Investigation Branch, Department of Trade and Industry, Room 323, Ashdown House, 123 Victoria St, London SW1E 6RB, tel. (071) 215 5000.

Overseas companies

Companies that are incorporated outside the UK but trade in this country (excluding the Isle of Man and the Channel Islands) are required to comply with certain sections of the Companies Acts.

Within one month of establishing a place of business within the UK, an overseas company must file the following information with Companies House:

- the memorandum of association and articles of association, or a certified copy of the company's charter
- a list of its directors and company secretary
- the name and address of its British representative (e.g. a solicitor or accountant) where legal documents can be served

An overseas company must also lodge its annual accounts with the Registrar of Companies. These are available for public inspection, and the Companies House microfiche can be obtained in the same way as for UK companies.

Annual reports

Many companies, particularly those that are conscious of their public image, publish annual reports which will set out some or all the following information:

- a summons for the annual general meeting
- the directors' and chairman's report

- the profit-and-loss account
- the balance sheet
- details of the parent company or subsidiary and associated companies
- the auditors' report

Some reference libraries stock copies of company annual reports. Otherwise, it is usually possible to obtain a copy by phoning the company's head office and asking the public relations department to send you a copy. The information obtained from the annual report may be sufficient to prevent the need for a visit to Companies House.

Other sources of information

Business directories

A journalist in Derbyshire telephoned the head office of a chemicals company asking for the name of the managing director and the year that the company had been established. The reply came back that both pieces of information were 'confidential as the information may assist our competitors'. The journalist was able to get the information simply by telephoning the reference library, as details of the company were readily available in business directories.

A mass of information on tens of thousands of companies is contained in the range of business directories available for consultation at main reference libraries. As much of the information is duplicated from one directory to another, libraries will often not hold them all. These are the main ones:

- *Who Owns Whom*. This is a very useful starting point in establishing if one company is a subsidiary of another. *Who Owns Whom* is divided into two volumes: Volume 1 lists in alphabetical order some 6500 parent companies and all of their subsidiaries; Volume 2 lists over 100,000 subsidiary companies and matches them up with their parent companies.
- *Directory of Directors*. This is another particularly useful basic reference book on business organizations. Volume 1 lists around 59,000 company directors who control Britain's major companies; for each individual, there is information on every company directorship held, together with details of whether they are executive or non-executive, chairman, managing director, etc. Volume 2 lists

some 16,000 major British companies and, for each, gives the full company name, area of business activity, names of directors, name of parent company and financial data.

- *The International Stock Exchange Official Year Book*. This profiles the nearly 4000 companies listed on the London Stock Exchange, and provides detailed information on each of them, including: registered office, head office, registrars, directors, auditors, bankers, registration history, principal subsidiaries, capital, loan capital, accounts, dividends, financial data. It also lists the Council of the International Stock Exchange, senior management, member firms and companies, and is the definitive guide to the working of the various financial markets.

- *Kelly's Business Directory*. Over 84,000 industrial, commercial and professional organizations in the UK are listed in this tome. Its 2404 pages are divided into three main sections: the White Pages, which provides a classified directory of manufacturers, merchants, wholesalers and firms offering services to commerce and industry; the Blue Pages, which provides an alphabetical index of those companies and firms; and the Yellow Pages, which covers international exporters and services.

- *Kompass*. This comprises two volumes which together contain over 5000 pages of detailed information on some 40,000 companies in the UK. Volume 1 lists details of these companies and the goods and services they offer. Volume 2 provides more detailed information on each, listed by county, including: address, office hours, names of directors and senior managerial staff, turnover, bankers, number of staff, product groups. It also states if the company is a member of the Confederation of British Industry (CBI).

- *Key British Enterprises*. Another hefty work – in three volumes totalling over 3000 pages – on what it describes as 'Britain's top 25,000 companies'. Volumes 1 and 2 list the companies in alphabetical order and provide information on location, business activity, trade names, parent company, directors, capital, sales, number of employees, etc. Volume 3 provides a products and services index, a trade index and a geographical index.

- *Sells Products and Services Directory*. Under 9500 classified headings are data on some 44,000 commercial and industrial companies in Britain, each entry giving full company name, description of business activity, address and phone numbers.

- **Macmillan Unquoted Companies**. An unquoted company is one that is not listed on the stock market. This directory lists some 10,000 unquoted companies, and identifies the head office address, business activity, directors, holding company, sales, profits, directors' emoluments, number of employees, employees' remuneration, audit fee, capital employed, net worth, profit margin and sales growth.

- **Crawford Directory of City Connections**. Despite its name, this directory lists a wide range of companies in and out of the City of London. Several thousand companies are included, including those on the Stock Exchange, the Unlisted Securities Market, the Over-the-Counter market and the Third Market as well as unquoted companies. It provides details of their stockbrokers, financial advisers, auditors, corporate solicitors, insurance advisers, public relations advisers, directors, senior executives, etc.

- **The City Directory**. Published by the Institute of Directors, it provides details on over 6500 companies under a number of headings including: the Securities and Investment Board and self-regulatory organizations; shipbrokers and air brokers; commodity and bullion markets; the money markets; banking sector institutions.

- **Who's Who in the City**. As its name suggests, *Who's Who in the City* lists the biographical details of more than 8000 prominent and senior City business personnel.

- **Business Information & the Public Library**. Although K.G.B. Bakewell's book is principally a guide to business information policy, it also contains an excellent guide to sources of business information, acting as a supplement to *Current British Directories*.

Specialist financial information

Hundreds of specialist financial publications appear every year, covering a diverse range of subjects from asphalt to zinc alloy products. The main source of information on such publications is the directory *Current British Directories* which lists some 250 local directories and 2500 specialist ones. The definitive library of specialist financial information in the UK is the British Library's Business Information Service (*see* Appendix 2). Otherwise the main specialist references are:

- **Extel**. Extel Financial Ltd publishes the Extel cards service, which is one of the most detailed sources of business information publicly available, covering more than 5500 UK firms. Many reference libraries stock Extel cards. Information provided includes: business of company, registration details, registration of securities, subsidiary and related companies, directors and officers, capital, directors' and other shareholding interests in the company, voting rights, dividends per share record, loan capital, profit-and-loss account, balance sheet, business analysis, geographical analysis, auditor's report, chairman's statement, financial calendar. Much of this information is obtained from the company's file at Companies House. Extel also periodically publishes 'news cards', which update the main annual card. Sample cards are available from Extel Financial Ltd, Fitzroy House, 13-17 Epworth St, London EC2A 4DL, tel. (071) 251 3333.

- **McCarthy**. McCarthy Information Services monitors the coverage on more than 3000 UK companies by more than 70 newspapers and periodicals. This is condensed on to a card system similar to the Extel cards, providing up-to-the minute information on many aspects of the companies activities. McCarthy also operates a weekly information service at £18 per company per year (minimum of five companies). This provides the subscriber with copies of any coverage of those companies from the 70 publications, on a weekly basis.

- *Financial Times* **Business Information**. The well-known pink newspaper provides a substantial range of business information on most sectors of the economy – but at a price. The FT Business Research Centre, which provides the most detailed business information, charges an annual membership fee of £295.00, a minimum annual deposit of £500.00, and an hourly research fee of £55.00 for the first hour and £27.50 for every subsequent hour. However, it does publish a wide range of financial publications at more-down-to-earth prices. Full details are available from: Financial Times Business Research Centre, 1 Southwark Bridge, London SE1 9HL, tel. (071) 873 3000.

- *The Bankers Almanac and Yearbook*. Volume 1 provides a very detailed profile on 3600 major international clearing banks and merchant banks trading in the UK, and outlines their histories, directors, officials, executives, regional directors, international services and overseas subsidiaries. Volume 2 is an international town-by-town guide of every branch of all the banks listed in Volume 1 – 146,000 branches in all.

- ***Building Societies Yearbook***. This lists every building society in the UK, including information on the directors, principal executives, head office, year of incorporation and number of branches. It also has sections on changes of name, members of the Chartered Building Societies Institute, a town guide of building society branches, and a directory of surveyors.

- ***Pension Funds and their Advisers***. Every major pension fund is listed in this directory, which gives information on their investments, capital value, annual contributions, annual investment income, number of members, pensioners, deferred pensioners, company employees, senior personnel, trustees, actuaries, solicitors, etc.

- ***Insurance Directory and Yearbook***. This publication comes in three volumes and provides 1571 pages of information on all aspects of the insurance world, including insurance companies, brokers, Lloyds syndicates, who's who, statistics.

- ***Investment Trust Yearbook***. Hundreds of investment trusts operate in the UK, and this yearbook supplies more than 500 pages of information, on each company and its investment strategy, including its principal investments, the distribution of those investments and details of its main shareholders.

- **Specialist trade directories**. Trade directories are used to indicate which companies supply particular products or services. They may also provide more detailed product and company information, and may cover one or a number of industries on a local, national or international level. Areas of coverage include: food, drink and tobacco; the chemical industry; oil and gas; transport, paper, printing and publishing; energy; leisure. The availability of such directories will vary considerably from library to library, but the key directories are listed in *Current British Directories*. The British Library Business Information Service (*see* Appendix 2) stocks most trade directories, and also houses a huge stock of market intelligence material.

Further information

A number of non-commercial organizations conduct research into various types of companies, and many publish their results. They include:

- **Labour Research Department (LRD)**, 78 Blackfriars Rd, London SE1 8HF, tel. (071) 928 3649. This is an independent trade union research organization (completely unconnected with the Labour Party) that publishes a number of reports on company profits, privatization, health and safety, employment law and related issues. LRD is particularly known for researching into political donations by British companies and the activities of right-wing pressure groups.

- **Centre for Alternative Industrial and Technological Systems (CAITS)**, 404 Camden Rd, London N7 0SJ, tel. (071) 607 7079/700 0362. CAITS is an independent research centre supplying information, advice and support to community groups, students, trade unions and local authorities. The research it conducts includes company profiles, sector analysis, social/economic audits, bargaining information and low-cost computerized business information. It also publishes a range of specialist reports.

- **Services to Community Action and Trade Unions (SCAT)**, 1 Sidney St, Sheffield S1 4RG, tel. (0742) 726683. SCAT undertakes a wide range of commissioned work on privatization, planning issues, tenants action and related issues for trade unions, local authorities and campaigning groups. They publish a large number of booklets and reports on privatization and contractors in the public sector.

- **Social Audit**, PO Box 111, London NW1 8XG, tel. (071) 586 7771. This has published a number of booklets on particular industries that are in some way controversial. For example, in 1985 it published the *Report on Investment in the UK Tobacco Industry*.

Useful books

Company Law by Colin Thomas ('Teach Yourself' Books published by Hodder and Stoughton in 1987). This guide provides a clear introduction to company law as it relates to the formation, financing, control and winding-up of business organizations in the UK, with reference to the Companies Acts and relevant case law. A very useful starting point for the financial novice, it incorporates the Companies Acts of 1980, 1981 and 1985.

Challenging the Figures by Christopher Hird (Pluto Press). Although published in 1983, this book is still an excellent and clearly written guide to dissecting company accounts. It explains, in lay person's language, how to interpret a company's accounts, how to work out what a company is investing, how it may be hiding profits and how near it might be to bankruptcy.

3 INVESTIGATING LOCAL AUTHORITIES

This chapter deals with such issues as housing, land, property, the air we breathe and the water we may – or may not – drink. Many things in these categories are regulated by local councils, and this chapter therefore covers all issues where there is a right to obtain information from local authorities or other municipal bodies.

However, this chapter also provides clear evidence of the absurdity of Britain having no cohesive and comprehensive Freedom of Information Act. Instead, what we have are numerous inconsistent and anomalous rights of access to information contained in a range of laws spanning many decades. For example, under the 1875 Explosives Act the public is freely entitled to inspect a register, kept by local councils, of premises where explosives are permitted to be stored. But although the same councils are also required to keep registers of those who possess firearms licences, no right exists for the public to inspect those particular registers.

Although this chapter details many of the legal rights we have to obtain official information from local government authorities, it is quite another thing to convince the bureaucrats to comply with their legal duty. There is substantial evidence that many local authorities frequently fail to make information available to the public. So how can the citizen make effective use of the 'right to know'?

Finding out general information

The first step is to find what information is readily available to the public, and become familiar with the structure of the council including the different areas of responsibility of the various committees and sub-committees. A visit to your local reference library is the appropriate place to start, as it should be able to provide a range of information including minutes of recent council meetings and the annual report or yearbook setting out details of the council's activities. Otherwise, the council information centre or Town Hall inquiry desk may provide details of publications and documents available to the public. Also, it should be possible during these visits to inspect notices giving details of forthcoming council and committee meetings, including their venues, dates and times.

'WHICH COUNCIL COMMITTEE DOES WHAT?' CHECKLIST
Different council committees do different jobs. This can be found out by:

- visiting the council's offices
- checking files in the local library
- looking at coverage of council meetings in the local press
- checking the *Municipal Yearbook*, which lists every local authority in the UK

A picture will soon emerge of which council committees deal with the issues you wish to investigate. Has the council already dealt with the issue, or is it something that is currently going through the council procedures? When will the public next be able to inspect audited accounts and the 'books, deeds, contracts, bills, vouchers and receipts' that accompany them? Do you now need to inspect background documents or registers?

Laws that give access to official information are very rare phenomena in Britain, and have so far received very little publicity. An application to the council from a member of the public to inspect documents will be quite an unusual event, so have patience with baffled local government officers who may have to find out from their superiors how to deal with such an eccentric request!

Sending off a clear letter to the appropriate council officer – or to the Chief Executive or Town Clerk if you are in any doubt – stating what information you would like to see may reduce the amount of 'confusion' that may arise. And remember, no reason has to be given about *why* that information has been requested. Any difficulties in obtaining information from a local authority should be referred to your ward councillor or, if necessary, to the local Member of Parliament.

The Municipal Yearbook

The main single source of information on local government is the *Municipal Yearbook* which covers the whole of the United Kingdom including various administrative oddities such as the Isle of Man, Channel Islands and the Isles of Scilly. The *Yearbook* comes in two bulky volumes which should be available in most principal reference libraries.

Volume 1 provides over 800 pages of facts about each function of local government and the responsibilities of local government officers. For example, it has detailed sections on civil defence, environmental health, social services, town and country planning, public relations, ombudsmen, police and probation services and so on. It also details a range of public utility services not strictly in the local government field, such as (currently) water authorities, national parks and ports authorities. It also lists the range of representative local authority associations.

Volume 2, which (in the 1989 edition) contains a further 940 pages, details every local government authority in the UK, and gives the name and address of all serving council members (councillors). Senior council officers are named, as well as other local public officials such as Lords Lieutenant (the Queen's local representatives), High Sheriffs and coroners. The idiosyncrasies of London government in the post-GLC era are clearly detailed, as are the various development corporations and other development bodies. Volume 2 also provides a useful guide to MPs, MEPs, central government departments, and key quangos.

The *Municipal Yearbook* is extremely thorough and detailed, well cross-referenced and indexed. It is undoubtedly the best starting point for any detailed research into local government or other municipal matters.

The Local Government (Access to Information) Act, 1985

In April 1986, this Act came into force, amending the 1972 Local Government Act, and is reproduced in Appendix 5. It opens up all Council committee and sub-committee meetings and gives the public access to agendas, reports, minutes and background papers – subject to a few strictly defined exemptions.

This is a unique 'right to know', unprecedented in English law, but because it is a complex piece of local government legislation (*see* Appendix 5 for the complete text), it can be quite offputting. For more information on the Act, the Community Rights Project booklet *Guide to Councillors' Rights to Information* (details on p. 37) is the definitive guide.

The Community Rights Project which drafted the Bill and campaigned for it to become law, has outlined the following as its main provisions:

- You have the right to attend meetings of the council and its committees and sub-committees (Sections 100A and 100E). These make important decisions affecting you.

- A council notice telling you about the meetings must be posted up at the main council offices at least three days in advance (Section 100A[6] and 100E).

- Before the meeting, you can see the agenda, reports to be presented and relevant internal documents, previously kept locked up in council filing cabinets (Sections 100B, 100D and 100E).

- If, during the meeting, you are asked to leave, you must be told exactly why; later you can read a summary of what was said (Section 100A[5], Schedule 12A, Section 100C).

- You can ask your local paper or a councillor to get more facts on an item on the agenda if it is not clear to you.

- All these agendas and reports are open to you for six years (Section 100C[1]).

- Important internal documents in the files are open to you for four years, (Section 100D[2]).

- You can find out from the main council offices the names and addresses of councillors and what committees and sub-committees they are on (Section 100G[1] and [4]).

- If a council officer is given power by councillors to take a decision on behalf of the council, you have the right to know who the officer is, and exactly what his or her duties and powers are (Section 100G[2] and [4]).

- The main council offices will have a list of your rights; this can be inspected during office hours (Section 100G[3] and [4]).

- You may have to pay to see internal documents (but *not* the reports, agendas or minutes) – but the charge must be reasonable (Section 100H).

- You can go to the main council offices during office hours and make a copy or photocopy of available information. Again, a reasonable fee may be charged (Section 100H).

- These rights also apply to other bodies such as the fire or police authority, joint committees of two or more councils, joint boards, etc. (Section 100).

- All the permitted reasons for keeping things secret are listed in the new law, and if you are prevented from seeing something, you must be told under which heading you are being barred. The council is not allowed to invent new headings or simply use terms such as 'confidential' or 'contrary to the public's interest' to deny you information. They can only use one of the specific reasons listed under the Act (Schedule 12A).

COUNCIL INFORMATION CHECKLIST 1

The Local Government (Access to Information) Act, 1985 allows you to:

- know about council meetings before they take place
- see committee agendas and minutes
- attend meetings of council committees and sub-committees
- obtain copies of background documents
- inspect and photocopy committee documents going back six years

COUNCIL INFORMATION CHECKLIST 2

You can be excluded from council meetings if genuinely confidential information is being discussed. But these rules must be followed:

- you must be told why you have to leave the meeting and what type of business is to be discussed
- the reason must be written in the minutes
- you must be allowed to return to the meeting afterwards
- councillors will be present and can make sure the rules are not being abused

Exemptions under the Act The specific categories of information expressly excluded under the Act are:

- Information relating to a particular employee or office-holder, former employee or office-holder, or job applicant.
- Information on occupiers of any council accommodation, or applicants for council accommodation.
- Information relating to any particular recipient of or applicant for any council service or financial assistance.
- Information regarding adoption, care, fostering or education of any particular child.

- Information relating to the business or financial affairs of any particular person (other than the local authority itself).
- The amount of any expenditure proposed to be incurred by the local authority under any particular contract for the acquisition of property or the supply of goods or services.
- The terms negotiated in contracts for the acquisition or disposal of property or the supply of goods and services.
- The identity of anyone tendering for council contracts.
- Industrial relations matters.
- Legal documents associated with legal proceedings by or against the council, or in relation with other forms of legal action or advice.
- Any action taken or to be taken in connection with the prevention, investigation or prosecution of a crime.
- The identity of protected informants.

Although this Act is quite clear about the information that must be made public, and that which is exempt under the law, there is little evidence to suggest that local authorities routinely comply with all their legal duties under this rare piece of freedom of information legislation. A survey carried out by the Community Rights Project in January 1987 revealed that, of the 450 local authorities questioned about compliance with the Local Government (Access to Information) Act, 'only a minority of councils have taken effective steps to ensure that all of their electors are aware of and understand their new rights; a far larger number keep quiet about the Act in the hope, presumably, that they will not have any more requests from the public for

---

Although the Local Government (Access to Information) Act provides wide access to local government documents, there are three major loopholes:

- It is left up to local councils how they publicize the Act, and some councils give the Act no publicity at all.
- Councils are permitted to charge 'a reasonable fee' to cover the costs of photocopying and inspection of documents. But there is no definition of 'a reasonable fee', and councils have charged £3.50 for one page of photocopying.
- The Act gives local authorities considerable powers to exclude information from its provisions, or discuss some matters in secret session.

information than before'. A story in a local Newcastle newspaper is all too typical: according to this, Newcastle City Council 'met in secret to discuss a confidential report congratulating them on how they conduct the city's affairs so openly'!

However, if a council officer fails to comply with the Act by, for example, denying a member of the public access to a background report, then a criminal offence is committed and the officer can be tried for it in the magistrates' court. Such breaches of the Act can be reported to the police, or, if there is one, to the local government ombudsman/woman through a local councillor. And don't forget that the press can be informed.

When is a committee not a committee?   One of the major problems that may confront an inquiring citizen pursuing their rights under this Act is the suggestion that certain council committees are not, in fact, committees at all. Rather they are 'groups' or 'working parties' and thus exempt from complying with the Local Government (Access to Information) Act.

In November 1988, the Court of Appeal ruled that individual councillors can be excluded from working parties as these groups were not committees or sub-committees of a council. But such groups can not make policies without them being submitted to a committee or sub-committee for approval, and any appropriate reports and background documents would then be available for inspection under the 1985 Act. However, closed groups have been seen to be 'sewing-up' decisions behind closed doors, and thus they deserve very close scrutiny.

How much can the Council Charge?   The 1985 Act allows local authorities to charge a 'reasonable fee' for supplying individuals with photocopies. Unfortunately, that term is not defined in law, and this has resulted in councils charging from nothing to £3.50 per sheet of photocopying.

Good practice

So far we have dealt with the minimum legal duties of local authorities under the Local Government (Access to Information) Act, 1985, but there is nothing to stop councils from doing more than they are required to under that Act. As we have seen, although the council can charge a 'reasonable' fee for photocopying, it can, if it wishes, provide the photocopies for free. Extending the citizens' rights in this way is called 'good practice', and councillors can make proposals for policies that will add to the good practices of the council.

On the other hand, if a council charges £3.50 for one page of photocopying – which isn't unknown – then that is clearly a bad practice, although apparently legal. If you experience bad practices – such as a lack of cooperation from council officers or any practices that prevent or deter members of the public from obtaining information – then these should be taken up with councillors and the local media.

The audit of council accounts

Under the Local Government Finance Act, 1982, each local authority must have its accounts audited annually by independent accountants. The Act also gives the public wide powers to 'inspect the accounts to be audited and all books, deeds, contracts, bills, vouchers and receipts relating to them and make copies of all or any part of the accounts and those other documents' (Section 17). In addition, the Act gives local government electors the right to challenge the accounts and question the auditor if a discrepancy or breach of legal duty is suspected.

FINDING OUT ABOUT THE AUDIT

- Ask the Treasurer's Department when the next audit will be.
- Check the 'Public Notices' columns in the local newspaper.
- Write in advance, saying you would like to inspect the accounts.
- Take along a list of the documents you want to see.
- Make a note of what happens in case you need to complain later.

The Accounts and Audit Regulations, 1983 (Statutory Instrument 83/1761) spells out in considerable detail the way in which the audit must be conducted, including a requirement that the council must advertise the right of public inspection once it is completed. A little advert will appear hidden away in the 'public notices' section of the local paper, so keep your eyes peeled – especially during the holiday period when many people go away. And remember that there is a tight timetable regulating the audit, and you have only a two-week period each year in which to inspect the accounts.

The Audit Commission, the government's watchdog on local government expenditure, has published *Local Government Audit Law* (HMSO), which at £19.50 is *the* authority on local government audits. The right to inspect detailed financial documents is one of the most powerful right-to-know provisions in local government law.

Section 228 (2) of the Local Government Act, 1972

This is an obscure and ill-defined piece of local government law – although potentially a very valuable one – which states that 'an elector for the area of a local authority may make a copy of or extract from an order for the payment of money made by the local authority'.

Unfortunately, the term an 'order for the payment of money' is not defined anywhere in the 1972 Act, and there have been no recent court cases to resolve the matter. However, you still have a right to inspect the orders for the payment of money – whatever they may be – and should find out from the council what they think this allows you to do. The logical point to argue is that an 'order for the payment of money' will be a written order from a council committee or senior officer to the finance department asking for the money to fund a particular transaction.

One tactic that can be used to test the water is to ask to see the 'orders for payment' that relate to a totally innocuous transaction – the purchase of minibuses by the education department, for example. Once you have established precisely what the council defines the term to mean, *then* you can ask the council to provide comparable documents in your own area of particular interest – the building of nuclear shelters, the purchase of firearms and ammunition by the local police authority, or whatever.

By-laws

These are local laws made by a council itself. For example, it may have passed a by-law to restrict or regulate the use of public spaces, or to lay down rules regulating the use of surveillance devices in public places. Copies of all by-laws must be deposited at the offices of the local authority that made them 'and at all reasonable hours be open to public inspection without payment'. Any person may purchase a copy of any by-law for a maximum of 20p, the price stipulated in Section 236 of the 1972 Local Government Act.

BY-LAWS CHECKLIST
Many councils make their own by-laws regulating council services and property, such as parks.

- Anyone can inspect the by-laws at council offices.
- They are usually available at the local libraries.
- Copies can also be bought from the council for no more than 20p each.

- All by-laws should be checked as they can give the public extra rights.

It is worthwhile looking through all of the local by-laws, as they may contain additional rights that will assist inquirers looking for detailed information on council business or may help people to put forward their point of view. For example, the London Borough of Haringey has a by-law allowing a deputation to address meetings of the council or its sub-committees, on the condition that at least ten days' notice is given, and that a memorandum is sent in advance stating the nature of the application. This is an effective way for individual members of the public or local groups to influence the decisions that affect their communities, and gain the attention of the local press.

Councillors' rights

As our elected representatives, councillors have an automatic right to information that may not be available to the public. Section 100F of the Local Government (Access to Information) Act states that a councillor may see any documents 'in the possession or under the control' of the council which 'contain material relating to any business to be transacted at a meeting of the council or a committee or sub-committee', unless those documents contain exempt information as outlined in Schedule 1 of the Act. These exemptions are similar to those listed on pp. 29–30 under 'Exemptions under the Act' but do not include financial and business affairs and expenditure under contracts.

WHAT YOUR COUNCILLOR CAN DO
Councillors are entitled to more information than the public. For instance, they can:

- inspect any document about council business, provided it does not contain certain categories of personal information.
- attend all council committee and sub-committee meetings, and the meetings of some working parties and groups.
- propose Standing Orders to the council, which will extend the public's rights of access.
- raise disputes about access to information at council meetings, which may then be publicized in the press.
- take a complaint about bad administration to the local government ombudsman/woman.

It is also held in common law that a councillor has the right to obtain a wide
– and unspecified – range of information on the working of the council,
although this does not give him or her a right to a 'roving commission'. An
idle curiosity is not a sufficient reason to inspect council files. The right exists
'so far as his access to the documents is reasonably necessary to enable the
councillor properly to perform his duties as a member of the council'. There
are fairly complex legal cases concerning the details of councillors' rights,
and these are covered in the Community Rights Project booklet, *Guide to
Councillors' Rights To Information.*

Councillors' expenses

It is a requirement for the council to 'keep records of all payments to members
[i.e. councillors] . . . indicating the amounts paid to each member and the
heading under which they were paid'. (Local Government [Allowances]
Regulations, 1974 [S.I. 74/447] as amended by the Local Government
[Allowances] [Amendment] [No. 2] Regulations, 1981 [S.I. 81/316].)

COUNCILLORS' EXPENSES CHECKLIST
The public can inspect records of expenses paid to local councillors, which
show:

- how much they were paid.
- of what committees they were members.
- what meetings they attended, and the dates.
- their membership of sub-committees.
- other activities for which they received payment.

Paragraph 5(2) of the 1981 Regulations states that the provisions of Section
228 of the 1972 Act applies where any local government elector for the area
of the local authority (or an appointed agent) may inspect records of payments 'at all reasonable hours'. In other words a local elector can inspect the
documents during normal office hours. As ever, a local government officer
who refuses to let a member of the public inspect the documents may be
breaking the law and can be prosecuted.

Election law

The Representation of the People Act, 1983 requires various documents and
accounts relating to local, parliamentary and European parliamentary elections and their candidates to be deposited with the Returning Officer. These

are available for public inspection under Section 89 of that Act and can reveal much about the local political parties and their candidates and officers.

ELECTION LAW CHECKLIST
Under election law, the public can inspect:

- literature used by candidates in local and parliamentary elections
- candidates' nomination papers
- financial returns of election expenses
- documents on election results

Data Protection Act, 1984

This Act (*see* p. 16) is useful when dealing with local government matters because huge amounts of information are held on computers by councils. The poll tax, housing, education, social services and the electoral register are examples of the departments that may have computerized files.

How the Data Protection Act can help with campaigning was demonstrated in October 1987 when an NCCL member wrote to the *Guardian* saying that an inspection of the *Data Protection Register* entry for the Kent Police computer had revealed that the police obtain information on 'suspects' from a frighteningly wide range of government departments, public bodies and local authority sources. These included: 'Inland Revenue, Customs & Excise, DVLC, Department of Education & Science, DSS, Department of Health, Department of Employment, Home Office, Ministry of Defence, local authority education departments, local authority social services departments, prosecuting authorities, hospitals, nursing homes, banks, lawyers, professional bodies, research organizations, workers, etc.' An inspection of the entries in the *Data Protection Register* for your local council and police force may prove very revealing.

Local government commissioner (ombudsman/woman) reports

Section 30 of the 1974 Local Government Act requires reports of investigations made by the local government commissioner (ombudsman/woman) to be made available for inspection, and to advertise the availability of the reports to the public in a local newspaper. The issues covered by the ombudsman/woman include complaints that have been made about the conduct of the council, particularly on maladministration – for example, when a council has failed to keep people informed of its decisions. And the commissioner has wide powers to obtain information and publish the facts in each case they investigate.

OMBUDSMAN/WOMAN CHECKLIST
A report by the ombudsman/woman (local government commissioner) of an investigation of a complaint against a local authority must be:

- sent to the person making the complaint.
- made available for public inspection without charge.
- advertised in a local newspaper.
- reported to the appropriate committee of the council.

Further information

The Community Rights Project is at the forefront of campaigning for open local government, and was responsible for steering the Local Government (Access to Information) Act through Parliament. It publishes a number of practical guides, including the *Access to Information Wallchart* (£1.00) and the *Guide to Councillors' Rights to Information* (£2.00), which is a must for anyone pursuing their rights to know.

Environmental issues

" There can be few trade secrets which are more important than the protection of the environment, and the protection of the lives of the public in the case of an industrial disaster, and the Association is apprehensive about the number of exemptions that are likely to arise.

Association of County Councils

Industry has insisted that its views on disclosure of information must themselves be kept secret. In 1986, the Department of the Environment issued a consultation paper which asked companies for comments on new proposals to publish air pollution statistics. Asked if they would allow the DoE to make their comments public, 381 of the 442 firms consulted – nearly 90 per cent of the total – refused. The secrecy permeating the final document means that even the names of these companies cannot be disclosed.

Fortunately for us there are many obscure laws requiring information on the environment to be made available for public inspection, in addition to other sources of published information.

Environment and Safety Information Act, 1988

This was introduced as a Private Members' Bill by Chris Smith MP, having been drafted and promoted by the Campaign for Freedom of Information. It requires safety and environmental authorities, including local councils and government departments such as the Health & Safety Executive, to set up public registers of the enforcement notices that have been served on factories, shops, railway stations, cinemas or other public places where breaches of safety and environmental laws have occurred. It became effective in April 1989.

> Two years after the King's Cross fire tragedy, a secret report commissioned by London Transport identified 126 fire risks – of which more than half were described as 'large' risks – at Tottenham Court Road station. The report was leaked to *Time Out* magazine. If it hadn't been, the public would not have known about the risks. The head of London Transport's safety operations said there was nothing in the report they wanted to hide, but he also said that releasing the report would have been 'counter productive'.

Integrated pollution control and local authority air pollution control: public access to information

This government consultation paper, published in September 1989, contains proposals requiring Her Majesty's Inspectorate of Pollution and local authorities to establish public registers giving: details of the issue of licences to companies involved in industrial pollution; a brief description of the process causing the pollution; details of variations of notices served by the enforcing authority; and information about any failures to comply with the conditions of the authorization. However, the proposals do contain a let-out clause so that companies will not have to declare 'commercially sensitive information'.

Air pollution and waste disposal

66 Rather than prescribe the information to which the public may have access, free access should be the first presumption . . . with free access to any information files held by the local authority.

Institution of Environmental Health Officers

Under Section 79 of the Control of Pollution Act, 1974, a register of information collected on air pollution by a local council environmental health department must be made available for public inspection. This law also deals with licences for waste disposal, which must also be kept in a register that is open to the public.

Highways, footpaths and bridleways

Section 57 of the Wildlife and Countryside Act, 1981 requires the surveying authority (usually the county or borough council) to compile and keep a copy of a 'definitive map' of not less than 1:2500 scale of 'all public rights of way in their area, classifying them as bridleways, footpaths or roads used as public paths'. This has to be made available for public inspection at all reasonable hours 'at one or more places in each district, and, where practicable, in each parish or community'.

Sections 15, 36 and 37 of the Highways Act, 1980, Section 215 of the Town and Country Planning Act, 1971 and Section 57 of the Wildlife and Countryside Act, 1981 also cover information on highways, by-ways and footpaths that must be available for inspection by the public.

Tree preservation

A register of tree preservation orders must be made available for public inspection under the provisions of the Town and Country Planning Act, 1971, as amended by the Town and Country Planning (Amenities) Act, 1972. A useful leaflet – *Protected Trees: a guide to tree preservation procedures* – is published free by the Department of the Environment and the Welsh Office.

TREE PRESERVATION ORDER CHECKLIST
The public is entitled to see the register of tree preservation orders, which shows:

- which trees have preservation orders.
- when the orders were made.
- who applied for the orders.
- who objected to them.
- why they were granted.

Further information

Books   A number of directories are available on environmental matters. *The Directory of the Environment* by Michael Barker, published by Routledge, is a 1400-page tome that covers a wide range of environmental organizations, from the Advisory Committee on Animal Experiments to Zoo Check. It also includes appropriate government departments, charities and campaigning groups, and contains lists of journals, a bibliography and a detailed subject index.

The Health and Safety Directory 1988/89, published by Kluwer, is the definitive guide to environmental policing, and provides details of every statutory body in the environmental health and public safety fields. All parliamentary and governmental agencies are listed together with appropriate local authorities.

Individual industries publish yearbooks that provide information on their activities. For example, the *Water Services Yearbook* gives details of each water authority and company and their personnel, together with information on the various government agencies, trade associations and institutions, and trade information and facts and figures. Similarly, the *Electrical Supply Handbook* gives detailed information on such organizations as the Atomic Energy Authority, nuclear inspectorate consultative committees, local electricity supply boards and so on.

The Green Pages: a directory of natural products, services, resources and ideas, published by Macdonald Optima, covers all manner of green and alternative issues. One chapter has sections on reference books, libraries, resource centres, advice centres, publishers, bookshops, directories, computer networks, etc.

Organizations *

- **The Open Spaces Society**. This is Britain's oldest national conservation body, and advises local authorities, voluntary bodies and the

* Addresses etc. for all these are contained in Appendix 1.

public on their statutory rights and how to exercise them. It publishes a number of excellent guides, action packs and information sheets on common land, rights of way, village greens and unclaimed land. Surprisingly, open spaces account for some 1.5 million acres of land in this country.

- **The Ramblers' Association**. The RA is primarily concerned with footpaths, and takes an active lead on the subject in campaigning against and formally opposing planning developments that threaten the landscape. It publishes a detailed leaflet entitled *Footpaths: rights of passage in the countryside*, as well as a number of 'Rights of Way' publications and 'Briefs for the Countryside'.

- **Council for the Protection of Rural England**. CPRE describes itself as 'the leading independent countryside conservation group' and has over 33,000 members in 44 county branches and 200 local groups throughout England. It acts as a centre for advice and information on matters affecting the planning, improvement and protection of the countryside, and publishes detailed briefings on the law and related issues.

- **Friends of the Earth**. On the investigative front, FoE publishes guides such as *The A–Z of Local Pollution: who to contact action guide* and *The Countryside Campaigner's Manual*.

> The Department of Transport has refused a Friends of the Earth researcher access to a copy of a report entitled *Safety of Cyclists: an analysis of the problem and inventory of measures to make cycling safer.* The DoT stated: 'Unfortunately we are unable to provide you with a copy of this report because it is a document restricted to representatives of the member nations. We should be pleased to help you on other cycling matters.' However, Friends of the Earth was able to obtain a copy from another source.

- **The Countryside Commission**. This is a government quango which publishes a most thorough and informative – and free – guide called *Out in the Country: where you can go and what you can do*, which explains the duties of landowners and the rights of the public. It also publishes the *Rights of Way Manual* (£5.00) – 'a do-it-yourself pack containing all the information and forms needed to carry out surveys of rights of way in the countryside'.

- **London Hazards Centre**. LHC's bi-monthly newsletter *The Daily Hazard* frequently covers the right-to-know aspects of environmental issues. Recent editions have referred to the Control of Pollution Acts and the Control of Industrial Major Accident Hazards Regulations.

Housing, land and property

Ownership of land

The ownership of all property, both commercial and domestic, is recorded by the Land Registry, but until 1 December 1990, that information will not be available for public inspection. From that date, however, the Land Registry Act comes into force, opening up the Land Registry for public inspection. All property built since 1925 has been registered at the Land Registry. Any built prior to that date will only be registered if it has been sold or transferred since. Anyone will have the right to inspect the entry on any property in the UK on payment of the appropriate fee – which has not yet been set. Further information can be obtained from the HM Land Registry, 32 Lincoln's Inn Fields, London WC2A 3PH.

It is possible to trace the history and past ownership of a property by grappling with local parish and county records offices. An expert in that field, Peter Bushell, has written a book on the subject – *Tracing the History of Your House* (£12.95) published by Pavilion Books.

Crown property

Although it may sometimes appear that the Crown is above the law, Crown property is required to comply with planning law in the same way as everyone else. This came as something of an embarrassment when, in 1983, the *Sunday Times* revealed that the Crown Estates Commission and the Crown's commercial property company, Greycoat Estates, had failed to obtain planning permission for hundreds of developments over a 12-year period. Parliament came to the rescue by rushing through face-saving legislation.

Housing matters

Sections 41, 43 and 44 of the Housing Act, 1980 provide local authority tenants with the right to have information made available to them on such matters as tenancy agreements, housing management, repairs, etc. Section 22 of the 1961 Housing Act requires a council to publish a register of houses in multiple occupation, and Section 63 of the Rent Act, 1977 makes it a legal requirement for a register of fair rents to be made available for public inspection.

COUNCIL HOUSING CHECKLIST
Local council tenants are entitled to information on:

- tenancy agreements
- housing management policy
- repairs policy
- the right to buy
- neighbourhood improvement schemes

Housing action areas

Section 36 of the Housing Act, 1974 permits a local authority to declare a 'housing action area'. If this happens, then under section 41 of the Act the council must make details of the scheme known to 'persons residing or owning property in the area'.

Housing associations

Any organization that is a housing association must register with the register of housing associations maintained by the Housing Corporation. Section 3 of the Housing Act, 1985 states: 'The register of housing associations shall be open to inspection at the head office of the Corporation [149 Tottenham Court Rd, London W1, tel. (071) 387 9466)] at all reasonable times.' It is equally reasonable to expect the local housing department to supply the information direct. Otherwise local campaigning groups in the housing sector, such as Shelter or a local advice centre, may be able to help obtain that information.

Land charges

The Land Charges Act, 1972 requires local councils to maintain a register of land charges (legal obligations that apply to a property) on all land and property in their area. For each property, the register will show such things as: whether the building is in a conservation area or a smoke control zone;

whether planning permission has ever been granted for any purpose; if the building is listed; if the road it is on has been adopted by the local council; if there are any footpath rights, tree preservation orders and the like. It does not, however, show the owner of the building. Local authorities can charge for an inspection of the land charges register, and some London local authorities charge £15 for *each* inspection of the register.

LAND CHARGES CHECKLIST
Each local authority keeps a register of land charges on every building, which reveals if:

- planning permission has been granted.
- any smoke control orders are in force.
- there are any environmental health problems.
- it is a listed building.
- it is in a conservation area.

Landlords

Under the Landlord and Tenant Act, 1987, most tenants have a right to know the name and address of their landlord. If the landlord is represented by an agent, such as a rent collector or managing agent, then the agent must supply the name and address of the landlord within 21 days of being asked. The landlord's name and address must appear on any written rent or service charge demand.

Land held by public bodies

Under Section 93 of the Local Government, Planning and Land Act, 1980, the Secretary of State for the Environment is enabled to compile and maintain a register of land holdings by public bodies, namely: county councils, district councils, London borough councils, the Common Council of the City of London, the Inner London Education Authority, joint authorities established under Part IV of the Local Government Act, 1985, the Commission for the New Towns, development corporations, the Housing Corporation, the British Airports Authority, the Civil Aviation Authority, British Shipbuilders, the British Steel Corporation, the National Coal Board (now British Coal), the BBC, the IBA, the Post Office, and various statutory undertakings, such as public utility authorities. It is not known if the Minister has compiled such a register. Although some of these bodies are no longer publicly owned, the Act still applies.

Section 96 of the 1980 Act requires the register to be available for public inspection 'at the council's principal office by any member of the public at all reasonable hours'. The register will detail all the property in that area belonging to those bodies. A charge may be made for photocopies of any information contained in the register.

Listed buildings

There are around 500,000 listed buildings in Britain. All buildings built before 1700 are listed, as are most of those dating from between 1700 and 1840 and those of 'definite quality and character' built between 1840 and 1914. Some selected houses built between 1915 and 1939 and a few outstanding buildings put up after 1939, such as the Royal Festival Hall, have now been accepted on to the Listed Buildings Register by English Heritage. Section 54 of the Town and Country Planning Act, 1971 requires a register of listed buildings for a particular area to be available for public inspection at the local planning department.

Rates register

Section 108 of the General Rate Act, 1967 entitles any ratepayer (of any area) to inspect a range of documents in relation to the rates, including valuation lists, notices of objection or appeal, and minutes of the assessment committee. However, such rates records do not necessarily identify the owner of a property. These provisions will continue for commercial and industrial premises once the poll tax (community charge) comes into effect.

Residential homes

The Register of Homes Act, 1980 requires social services departments to keep a register of homes for old people, disabled people and mentally ill people. The register must be available for public inspection.

Sewers

Section 32 of the Public Health Act, 1936 requires the local authority to make plans of sewers available for public inspection. This would normally be at the local district or borough council's planning or highways department.

Vacant and unused land

Part X of the Local Government Planning and Land Act, 1980 relates to unused or underused land. Under Section 95, the Secretary of State may compile a register of such land for any public body and in any area that s/he decides. Some local authorities publish such a register and this will vary from area to area.

Planning

66   We do not think that registers alone necessarily provide adequate access – the public should have access to files, correspondence and the minutes of meetings.

Town and Country Planning Association

Planning applications

A notice of any application for planning permission must, under section 26(3) of the Town and Country Planning Act, 1971, be displayed on the site of the land in question for a minimum period of seven days, and must state that a planning application has been made. If the property is in a conservation area, the council must place an advertisement in the local newspaper *and* place a notice on the site of the property (Section 28 [2]). The Department of the Environment and the Welsh Office publish a number of free guides to planning: *Planning Appeals: a guide*; *Local Plans: public local inquiries and Public Inquiries into Road Proposals: what you need to know*. These give detailed guidance of the planning law and are available from public libraries.

PLANNING APPLICATIONS CHECKLIST
Details of planning applications must be publicized by:

- displaying a notice on the property.
- placing an advertisement in the local newspaper, if the property is in a conservation area.
- notifying immediate neighbours.
- making planning committee decisions available for public inspection.
- placing the application on a register for public inspection.

Under Section 34(1) of the 1971 Act, the application must also be kept on a public register, together with detailed information such as plans and the planning authority's decision. This has to be available for public inspection 'at all reasonable hours'. Section 92A of that Act also makes it a duty to keep a register of all enforcement and stop notices (which are notices made against people who carry out development without planning permission).

Until recently, although it has been possible to inspect planning applications it has not been possible to make copies of the documents without the permission of the architect or developer. However Section 47 of the Copyright, Design and Patents Act, 1988 states: 'Material open to public inspection pursuant to a statutory requirement may be copied with the authority of the appropriate person' (i.e. the planning officer). Subsection 2 of the Act confirms that copying is allowed 'for the purposes of enabling material to be inspected at a more convenient time and place'.

Structure plans.

A structure plan is a detailed series of proposals that the local authority is required to draw up under section 7 of the Town and Country Planning Act, 1971 to specify the 'development and other use of land in that area including measures for the improvement of the physical environment and the management of traffic, etc.'

Section 8 of the 1971 Act specifically requires councils to give 'adequate publicity' to their surveys *prior* to drawing up structure plans and give the local people the right to air their views on the proposals. The subsequent structure plan would then become a public document – not least under the Local Government (Access to Information) Act as a background document of a council's planning committee.

Regulations 36-39 of the Town and Country Planning (Structure and Local Plans) Regulations, 1982 (82/555) make certain documents, prepared by local authorities *outside* London in connection with structure and local plans, available for public inspections. In London it is the Town and Country Planning (Local Plans for Greater London) Regulations, 1974 (74/1481) that apply.

Further information

- **The Town and Country Planning Association** provides free and independent town planning advice to community groups, residents associations and individuals who are unable to afford a planning consultant. The TCPA sponsors the agency 'Planning Aid for

London' which publishes an excellent range of community manuals on planning, including *A Short Guide to Understanding Planning Jargon and the Planning System*, and *Resisting the Wreckers*.

- **Transport 2000** publishes a number of guides on the transport aspects of planning, including the *Objector's Guide to Trunk Road Inquiries*.

Civil Defence

Local authorities have had a statutory responsibility for civil defence since 1937. They are under an obligation to make plans, build emergency centres, recruit volunteers, train staff and take part in exercises. The structure of the civil defence authorities – usually county councils – is specified in the *Municipal Yearbook*. In London, the responsibility lies with the London Fire and Civil Defence Authority (LFCDA). All the organizations involved are local government authorities and therefore have to comply with the Local Government (Access to Information) Act, local government audit regulations and the like.

CIVIL DEFENCE CHECKLIST
Details of civil defence arrangements must be made available for public inspection, including:

- background documents
- agendas of the local civil defence committee
- minutes of their meetings
- accounts at their annual audit

The public also has the right to attend the meetings of the local civil defence committee.

However, more often than not, the concerned citizen runs into the brick wall of secrecy. A woman who lived near the Hinckley Point nuclear power plant became worried about the apparent lack of any evacuation arrangements should there be a major accident at the plant. She thought that worried parents trying to evacuate their children from the area might clog the roads. When she asked the chief constable if there were any contingency plans, she was told that there were – but they were confidential.

Fortunately, there are two organizations that can give some advice and information on civil defence:

- **The Emergency Planning Information Centre** (formerly the London Nuclear Information Unit), which campaigns for a safe nuclear-free environment, was established by a number of London boroughs following the abolition of the Greater London Council (GLC). It publishes free guides on civil defence, nuclear London and the transportation of nuclear materials by train.

- **The University of Bradford School of Peace Studies** was set up in 1973 and operates the only Peace Studies degree course in the United Kingdom. Areas of research include labour relations, the politics of disarmament, alternative defence strategies, international resource conflict, the development of peace movements and aspects of the conflicts in Northern Ireland and the Middle East. It has published a number of 'Peace Studies Papers' on civil defence.

Education

Educational establishments

Education in the UK is provided by a wide range of organizations in the public and private sectors, including charities, trusts, religious organizations, local state education authorities and private companies (for example, Winchester Public School, Cheltenham Ladies College, most polytechnics and no fewer than 26 of Oxford's 28 colleges are registered as private companies).

If it is necessary to conduct thorough research on an educational establishment, it may be useful to check the Companies House Index, Registry of Friendly Societies, Index of Charities and the mass of publications available in public libraries on every conceivable educational establishment.

Otherwise, the principal reference source on educational institutions is the *Education Yearbook*. This is an extremely thorough guide to educational organizations throughout the UK both in the public and private sectors. Its 740 pages cover government departments, local education authorities, examining bodies, teachers' organizations, research and advisory bodies, employment and careers, physical education and sport, denominational education bodies and so on.

The Education Authorities Directory and Annual is a useful alternative, providing detailed information on the statutory education bodies and local education authorities, together with a list of every secondary and middle school in the country. It also has chapters on further education, polytechnics, universities, special schools, etc.

Hundreds of handbooks have been published on educational establishments and the courses offered. For example, if you need to obtain detailed information on a public school, the place to look is the *Independent Schools Yearbook 1989* (of which two editions are published – one for boys' schools and one for girls'). For instance, the entry on world-famous Harrow details the names of the governors, headmaster, assistant masters, house tutors and support staff, and gives information on admission criteria, scholarships, fees (£2,725 per term), organization and curriculum and school societies.

The *University of London Calendar* is an example of the information available on a university. The handbook – or prospectus – lists each faculty, school and department in the University of London, together with a list of key departmental personnel. The structure and membership of the Court, the Senate, the Committee of the Senate, the Convocation and the various committees and sub-committees are detailed. This is representative of the information that should be available on all major academic institutions.

EDUCATION CHECKLIST

A wide selection of information is available on schools and colleges. The main directories are:

- *Education Yearbook*
- *Education Authorities Directory and Annual*
- *Independent Schools Yearbook*
- *Municipal Yearbook*
- college and university prospectuses

Education policy

The 1980 Education Act imposes on local education authorities (i.e. the county councils and metropolitan borough councils) a duty to publish information on arrangements they make for admissions of pupils to their schools and various other such arrangements. This has effectively been replaced by the provisions of the Local Government (Access to Information) Act, which makes all background papers and reports available to the public; therefore the public should be able to obtain documents on all aspects of local education policy.

School records

Records kept on pupils are secret, and some of the information and comments they contain can be very misleading. Here are some examples:

- 'Immature' (used to describe a child of seven).
- 'Religion is Mormon, it hasn't helped the situation.'
- 'She has vicious tendencies' (a girl of nine; her next teacher failed to find them).
- 'X has a reputation for petty theft, which we are sure of, but there is lack of evidence in several cases.'

Marie Macey of Bradford University attempted to carry out some research into school record-keeping. She wrote to 42 local education authorities asking for basic information, such as copies of the blank forms on which records about pupils were kept. The majority of those contacted categorically refused to supply even the most innocuous information.

Social services

The most thorough guide to social services is the *Social Services Yearbook*. Its 806 pages contain sections on the following: social services legislation; parliamentary committees handling social service issues; the Departments of Health and Social Security; the prison services; the probation service; health authorities and councils; community health councils; community relations; voluntary organizations; advice and counselling; professional bodies; research and development. The *Yearbook* details each social services department in the UK, and lists its head office, principal offices and area offices and officers.

66   The Secretary of State shares the increasingly held view that people receiving personal social services should, subject to adequate safeguards, be able to discover what is said about them in social services records.

DHSS Circular LAC(83)14 1983

The only specific piece of legislation requiring disclosure of information about the social services is section 1(2)(a) of the Chronically Sick and Disabled Persons Act, 1970, which requires all the social services departments of the county and metropolitan borough councils to publicize general information regarding their provision of services for the blind, deaf and handicapped or disabled. Otherwise, the Local Government (Access to

Information) Act, 1985 provides a general right of access to social service departments in the same way as for education matters.

Miscellaneous

Clubs

Private clubs that sell intoxicating liquor are required to register under the 1964 Licensing Act. Section 51 requires the clerk to the justices at the local magistrates' court to keep a register of clubs holding registration certificates, which any member of the public is entitled to inspect.

Crematoria

The Directory of Crematoria lists, by county, each crematorium in the UK and gives details of the name of the operator, the superintendent and registrar of each site, the ownership structure, an outline of the law on crematoria and a surprisingly detailed range of facts and figures on the subject.

Direct labour organizations

Under section 18 of the Local Government Planning and Land Act, 1980, any local authority that operates direct labour schemes must publish an annual report to be available for public inspection. Its publication must be announced in an advertisement in at least one local newspaper, together with details of where it can be inspected or bought and at what cost.

DIRECT LABOUR CHECKLIST
Local councils have a duty to publish information on direct labour organizations that carry out:

- refuse collection
- cleaning of buildings
- other types of cleaning
- school and welfare meals catering
- other types of catering
- maintenance of grounds
- repair and maintenance of vehicles

The Local Government Act, 1988 was enacted with the intention of making many local government services 'competitive', including the collection of refuse, cleaning of buildings, school and welfare catering, maintenance of grounds, and the repair and maintenance of vehicles. Section 12 of the Act deals with the publication of information about such work, including detailed financial information on competitive bids for contracts.

Explosives

Each local authority – in this case, each district or borough council – is required under the 1875 Explosives Act to keep a register of 'store licenses'. These are licenses for premises where explosives are stored, and for a fee of 5p, any local ratepayer is entitled to inspect the register. (In the post-poll tax era, councils will probably consider that any community charge payer or anyone whose name appears on the electoral register to be the replacement of the 'ratepayer'.)

Gambling

Under Schedule 1, paragraph 34 of the Betting, Gaming and Lotteries Act, 1963, a committee of 5–15 local justices of the peace is required to keep registers of all bookmakers' permits, betting agency permits and betting office licences – to be made available during reasonable hours for inspection by any constable or, on payment of the prescribed fee, any other person. Schedule 4, paragraph 3 requires the licence to be displayed on the appropriate premises by the bookmaker. Schedule 10 of the Gaming Act, 1968 requires the licensing authority of gaming clubs and premises with gaming machines to maintain a register of licences for public inspection. Inquiries should start at the local magistrates' court office.

GAMBLING CHECKLIST
Anyone can inspect public registers detailing:

- bookmakers' permits
- betting agency permits
- betting office licences
- gaming club licences
- gaming machine licences

Health and Safety at Work Act, 1974

Section 2(c) of this Act requires all employers to make 'the provision of such information, instruction, training and supervision as is necessary to ensure, so far as is reasonably practicable, the health and safety at work of [their] employees'. Trade unionists and other employees, therefore, may have direct access to information that might otherwise be withheld from the public.

For instance, shop stewards at a Gillingham hospital were able to obtain information on hazardous chemicals routinely handled by ancillary staff by using rights to information disclosure under the Health and Safety at Work Act, 1974. Previously, health service officials had refused to provide that information to members of the district health authority, as they had no obligation to do so.

HEALTH AND SAFETY CHECKLIST
Information must be made available to employees on:

- hazards at work
- instruction on hazards
- staff safety training
- supervision of health and safety
- fire regulations and first aid provisions

Pipelines

Under Part I of the first schedule to the Pipelines Act, 1962, anyone planning to construct any kind of pipeline – gas, oil, water or sewage – must publicize their proposals to 'those persons inhabiting land in the vicinity of the route of the proposed pipeline'. This usually entails placing an advertisement in the 'public notices' section of local, regional or national newspapers. The notice will state where the plans of the proposed pipeline can be inspected, which will probably include the local planning authority (the district or borough councils) with which copies of the plans have to be deposited.

Pubs

Section 34 of the Licensing Act, 1964, applies to the ordinary pub on-licences and off-licences. An off-licence is a shop licensed to sell alcohol for consumption off the premises. An on-licence is a licence to sell alcoholic drinks for consumption on the premises – such as in a pub or club. A register of licences is available for inspection by 'any person rated in respect of a hereditament in the district' – in other words, any local resident. Section 183 requires a sign to be fixed to the premises 'in a conspicuous place' naming the licensee and stating if the licence is an on-licence or an off-licence.

PUBS AND CLUBS CHECKLIST
Registers are available for inspection at magistrates' courts showing:

- details of publicans with on-licences
- details of off-licence holders
- private members' clubs
- occasional licences
- licence extensions

Sex shops

These are regulated under the Local Government (Miscellaneous Provisions) Act, 1982, which requires notices of applications for sex shop licences to be published in a local newspaper.

Ships

The 1989 *Lloyd's Register of Shipping* provides details of the 76,000 or so ships registered with Lloyd's. The four volumes provide information on country of origin, owners, former names, port of registry, tonnage, classification, ship type/cargo facilities, on-board machinery, etc.

4 INVESTIGATING HEALTH SERVICES

The National Health Service is a huge bureaucracy with a legal structure and bureaucratic culture that bears no resemblance to those of any other governmental organization – local or national. Attempting to obtain information on or from a health authority can be a complex process fraught with misunderstandings. The matter is not helped by government proposals for yet further reforms of the health service structure and the way in which health services are to be delivered – controversial proposals that form draft legislation currently being considered by Parliament.

Although the principal responsibility of the NHS is to care for the health of the public, its bureaucracy is not exempt from the obsessive levels of secrecy that exist in almost every institution in the land. This is clearly demonstrated in a survey published by the Association of community health councils in England and Wales (ACHCEW) in 1986 entitled *Information Needs of Community Health Councils*. A number of Community Health Councils (CHCs) – our independent watchdogs in the NHS – reported that requests for information from district health authorities were either met with lengthy delays or outright refusal. Some CHCs were refused information and documents by their district health authorities that were sent out routinely by others. Medway CHC in Kent, for example, could not obtain basic information about waiting lists, and after Haringey CHC in London was refused information on waiting times at Accident and Emergency Departments, a survey on the issue by the health authority, which had not previously been published, was only made available once the CHC announced that it would conduct its own survey.

ACHCEW identified a number of areas where information provision is inadequate:

- a lack of information on health planning proposals.
- insufficient financial information.
- poor timing of the release of crucial information.
- details of hospital closures not given in time to enable CHCs to propose making alternatives.
- a lack of details of complaints received by district health authorities.
- a lack of waiting list statistics.
- a lack of full papers from relevant medical and planning committees.

In other words, anyone wishing to obtain information from the NHS may have to spend quite some time pressurizing the bureaucrats in order to succeed.

It is not only the NHS bureaucracy that is unwilling to operate in the public eye: the private sector can be equally evasive. In January 1989, members of the Hillingdon Health Authority in Greater London were threatened with legal action if they disclosed any information about Bioplan Holdings, a company that runs private hospitals, after the health authorities had signed a strict confidentiality agreement as part of a contract with Bioplan to develop jointly a 50-bed private hospital.A member of Hillingdon Health Authority, Tony Rodgers, told the *Health Service Journal* that he had not been allowed to see a report commissioned by the health authority about the company. He said: 'I am concerned about the overall nature of Bioplan and I want to see the information on the background of the company. I am not going to sign the agreement.'

At the same time, officers at Eastbourne Health Authority in East Sussex recommended a Bioplan package to the authority's members. The deal included a contribution of £250,000 towards an operating theatre at Uckfield if the health authority agreed to spend £4.5 million on a new joint hospital venture. So, where should the inquiring citizen commence his or her research of the National Health Service and the private sector?

National Health Service

The most thorough guide to the complexities of the public health sector, and thus the starting point of any research, is the *Hospitals and Health Services Yearbook*. This 1000-page tome covers every aspect of the health service: the appropriate government departments and statutory bodies; health service finance; health service law; organizations; the independent sector; Ministry of Defence hospitals; special hospitals.

A section on each district health authority includes: the senior members and officers; the location of each hospital, including details of the type of hospital and bed capacity; community care provision; health centres; schools of nursing; ambulance services; and community health councils.

Community health councils

The local community health council (CHC) – a network of independent consumer councils set up by the government in 1974 to monitor and review the health service and to recommend improvements – is the citizen's closest ally when it comes to dealing with the NHS. In Scotland, the equivalent bodies are the local health councils; in Northern Ireland, the district committees. CHCs have a legal duty to represent the interests of the community in the NHS. The Community Health Councils (Access to Information) Act, 1988, brings CHCs in line with the requirements of the Local Government Act, 1972, which provides a right of public access to the meetings and documents of certain authorities. Each CHC is expected to cover all aspects of the NHS and has a legal right to:

- be consulted by the health authority or family practitioner committee (*see below*) on any substantial development or variation of NHS services.
- obtain a wide range of information from the NHS.
- receive comments from the health authority and family practitioner committee on its annual report.
- set up formal meetings with the health authority and family practitioner committee.
- send an observer to health authority and family practitioner committee meetings.
- enter and inspect NHS premises.

It is the legal duty of each CHC to:

- keep under review the operation of the health service in its district and make recommendations for the improvement in that service.
- publish an annual report detailing its activities.

There are some 215 CHSs in England and Wales – roughly one per health district. They have between 18 and 24 members drawn from the local community: half are nominated by the local council; one-third are elected by local voluntary organizations; and the remainder are appointed by the regional health authority. CHC members are voluntary and unpaid, and are supported by a staff usually numbering no more than two.

COMMUNITY HEALTH COUNCIL CHECKLIST
The local CHC can help members of the public by:

- finding out information on the NHS.
- observing meetings of the district health authority.
- entering and inspecting NHS premises.
- helping patients with complaints.
- putting forward suggestions for improvements.

Your local community health council will be able to assist with any research on local health services, particularly if you need information about the district health authority and family practitioner committees, their meetings and officers. The CHC is also uniquely placed to advise on complaints procedures and campaigning around specific health issues.

Local CHCs have a number of leaflets and other publications available for consultation. The Association of Community Health Councils in England and Wales publishes a number of guides on the health service, including:

- *The Public and the NHS: a report on public accountability in the NHS and the role of CHCs* (£3.00)
- *A Directory of Community Health Councils* (£5.00)
- *Bibliography of CHC Publications* (£1.00)

Address: The Association of CHCs in England and Wales, 30 Drayton Park, London N5 1PB, tel. (071) 609 8405.

College of Health

Another organization that publishes guides on health service information is the charity, the College of Health. Its publications on the subject include:

- *Consumer's Guide to Health Information* (£3.95)
- *Informing Health Consumers: a review of health information needs and services* (£5.00)

The College of Health pioneered the publication of information on hospital waiting lists for operations, and its *Guide to Hospital Waiting Lists* is now in its sixth edition (£5.00). The College also keeps a computerized register of over 1200 self-help groups and voluntary organizations for people who suffer from particular diseases, disabilities and handicaps. It also pioneered the magazine *Self Health* which is now published by the Consumers' Association as *Which? Way to Health*, which contains a great deal of information about the health services.

Address: The College of Health, 18 Victoria Park Square, London E2 9PF, tel. (081) 980 6263.

The British Medical Association

"   We support the right of patients and clients to have access to all information which is held about them on their behalf. Such access encourages openness and can improve the quality of the record by correcting factual errors and reducing misunderstandings.

May 1983 Report of an interprofessional working party set up by the BMA

On the subject of campaigning organizations, it is worth mentioning here the British Medical Association. The BMA is effectively the doctors' trade union, and is one of the most vigorous campaigning organizations concerned about, and critical of, the government's proposed reforms of the NHS. It publishes a range of literature on the subject and can be contacted at BMA House, Tavistock Square, London WC1H 9JR.

The equivalent organizations for dentistry and eye care are the British Dental Association, 64 Wimpole St, London W1M 8AL, tel. (071) 935 0875; and the General Optical Council, 41 Harley St, London W1N 2DJ, tel. (071) 580 3898.

The health service ombudsman

The health service ombudsman – or health service commissioner, as this job title is officially known – has a duty to investigate the administration of complaints against regional health authorities, district health authorities, family practitioner committees, boards of governors, the Public Health Laboratory Service Board and certain special health authorities established by the Secretary of State to carry out special functions. There are separate health service ombudsmen for England, Wales and Scotland.

The ombudsman does not investigate the complaints themselves, but will become involved if, for example, the third letter of complaint to a hospital administrator is ignored, or no action has been taken about a complaint. Your local community health council can advise on the use of the ombudsman scheme.

The scheme is itself indicative of the inconsistent approach on information that prevails in this country. While reports by the local government ombudsman must be made available for public inspection, and a notice of their publication must be placed in the local press, no such requirement is made of the health service ombudsman. There is a duty for a copy of the report to be lodged with the district health authority or family practitioner committee and with the complainant, but no requirement for it to be made public. Often the ombudsman's annual report to Parliament is the first time that many of the complaints against the NHS are made public.

Details of the health service ombudsmen are available from:

- *For England*: Church House, Great Smith St, London SW1P 3BW, tel. (071) 212 7676
- *For Wales*: 4th Floor, Pearl Assurance House, Greyfriars Rd, Cardiff CF1 3AG, tel. (0222) 394621
- *For Scotland*: 2nd Floor, 11 Melville Crescent, Edinburgh EH3 7LU, tel. (031) 225 7465.

District health authorities

As we saw earlier in this chapter, the investigating citizen's closest ally is the local community health council, which has a statutory right to obtain information on the district health authority. But there is some information that the public can obtain in their own right:

- The meetings of each district health authority are governed by the Public Bodies (Admission to Meetings) Act, 1960, which requires the meeting to be open to the public – although there is no provision requiring any documents to be made available. The press and public can be excluded from a meeting only by a resolution of the meeting. This usually covers the part of the agenda that deals with legitimately confidential business, such as complaints, personnel matters, etc. Any query should be directed to the district administrator at the district health authority's headquarters. The address and phone number will be found in the telephone directory under the name of the district health authority.
- Some health authorities and local councils operate joint committees on aspects of health care provision, such as community care. Such

committees are bound by the Health Service Joint Consultative Committees (Access to Information) Act, 1986, which brings joint committees in line with the Local Government Act, 1972, as amended by the Local Government (Access to Information) Act, 1985. All meetings of these committees are required to be open to the public, and background reports, agendas and lists of the committee members are to be made available. This presents another major anomaly in British law – more information is available about a joint committee than about a health authority. Also, unlike local government authorities, there is no legal right to inspect health authority accounts at the time of audit; therefore, the public has no parallel right to scrutinize documents that relate to financial transactions.

• The only other legal requirement on the health authority to make information available to the public is in the Hospital Complaints Procedure Act, 1985, where under section 1(b) the health authority must publicize their arrangements for dealing with complaints.

Family practitioner committees

These are the bodies responsible for administering and supervising the services carried out under NHS contracts by GPs, dentists, opticians and pharmacists. In Scotland, the equivalent is the Area Health Board and, in Northern Ireland, the Central Services Agency. They publish lists of doctors, dentists, opticians and pharmacists for each area, which are available for public inspection.

The family practitioner committees are, like district health authorities, also required to comply with the provisions of the Public Bodies (Admission to Meetings) Act, 1960, and allow the press and public to attend meetings.

Private health care

The private sector has been a growth area in recent years, and legislation currently under consideration will allow hospitals to opt out of the traditional health service structure. Some have set up as private companies to cover this eventuality. St Bartholomew's, the Royal Free, Guy's Hospital and the Royal Northern are among the London hospitals that are now registered companies; others will no doubt follow.

There are a number of sources of information on the private sector:

- *Directory of Independent Hospitals and Health Services.* Part I of this thorough reference book outlines the law as it relates to private health services, and has an informative chapter on private practice. It also lists the hospitals, homes and organizations that belong to the Association of Independent Hospitals.

  Part II lists every private hospital in the UK, and gives details of the owner, senior staff and number of beds. This part also identifies the number of pay beds in each NHS hospital; and lists all nursing homes, private homes and voluntary homes by county. An 80-page index lists every institution mentioned in the directory.

- *Laing's Review of Private Healthcare* is another directory of the private healthcare sector, covering the same categories of information as the *Directory* in its 1238 pages.

- Perhaps the most revealing source of information on organizations in the private sector will be Companies House (*see* pp. 16–17). Like any other private or public limited company, those in the health sector are required to file a considerable amount of detailed information. Therefore Bioplan Holdings will find itself in some considerable difficulty in maintaining the secrecy that it has sought. A large proportion of the private sector organizations are companies, the remainder being friendly societies (*see* p. 72) or charities (*see* p. 70).

Complementary/alternative medicine

The various forms of complementary/alternative medicine, such as homoeopathy and osteopathy, are booming areas although there is no legislation to control or regulate such practices. *The Institute of Complementary Medicine Yearbook* lists the dozens of self-regulatory bodies involved in anything from Acupuncture to Zone Therapy. The information service at the Institute for Complementary Medicine provides 'information on all aspects of complementary medicine' and can be contacted on (071) 636 9543. *The Directory of Complementary and Alternative Practitioners*, published by Health Farm Publications, lists many practitioners in these fields.

Central government

The government and its agencies, such as the Department of Health, retain much of the responsibility for planning health care provision in the UK. The ombudsman can have an impact on local health services, although s/he reports directly to Parliament. Therefore any detailed research into health service policy should include a search of reports published on the subject by the government. This is achieved by checking the index of the *HMSO Monthly Catalogue* (*see* p. 94).

However, the government only reluctantly lets go of its secrets – even when risks to health are involved. For four years, government health experts met in secret and decided to take no action on American evidence that aspirin could be fatal to children under the age of 12 – while the boffins waited to see if the same effect was occurring in Britain. During this period, 229 children developed Reyes syndrome, a condition which is now acknowledged to be linked with the use of aspirin. About half of those children died.

5 INVESTIGATING THE VOLUNTARY SECTOR

The voluntary sector covers a wide range of formal and informal organizations at a local, regional, and national level, ranging from multi-million-pound charitable bodies such as Oxfam to a small, local collective that may have a single purpose. Many of these bodies, whether or not they have official status, influence the society in which we live in one way or another. For example, the number of groups that sprang up in 1989 to oppose the proposed route of the Channel Tunnel railway link – a campaign that forced a major government policy rethink – demonstrates the way in which *ad hoc* groups at a local level can influence major social policy decisions.

However, investigating such organizations is no easy task. Although it is possible to research voluntary groups and organizations, information may have to be obtained from a number of formal and informal sources that will vary from one case to another.

Anyone conducting research into an organization will probably have a clear idea of what information is being sought. But the following checklist may help with planning an investigation:

- Who runs the organization? Who sits on the main committee or board?
- Who are the principal individuals in the organization and what are their other activities and interests?
- Who makes up its membership? Do they represent other organizations or bodies?
- What are the aims and objectives of the organization?
- What are its major policies?
- Where does the organization meet, and how often?

- Are there any paid officials? Who are they?
- Does the organization obtain publicity? Is it involved with the local press and broadcast media?
- Is the organization part of a local, regional, national or even international network?

Some groups in this category will be open organizations that present their views publicly and conduct their work in the full light of day – local amenity groups, for example, have a very public presence. But there are other organizations that wield power behind closed doors and are perceived, rightly in many cases, as being very secretive.

An example of that secrecy – and a useful example of the techniques to be used when conducting research into voluntary groups and organizations – is the world of Freemasonry. *The Masonic Yearbook*, effectively an unpublished manual, is crammed with details about every Masonic lodge and chapter in the UK, numbering something in excess of 12,500 individual groups. The list of Masonic lodges provides a detailed insight into the Masonic influence in our society. London alone has 1676 lodges and 704 grand chapters, some of which have names that reveal the nature of their membership: Athenaeum (lodge no. 8415); Bank of England (263); Barbican (8494); Certified Accountants (3162); City University (7962); Guildhall (3116); Household Brigade (2614); London Mayors (3560); National Artillery (2578); National Westminster (3647); Old Etonian (4500); Portcullis (6085); Public Schools Installed Masters (9077); Radio Fraternity (8040); Royal Air Force (7335); Royal Albert Hall (2986); Royal Dental Hospital (7099); Savoy (8356); South Africa (6742); Telephone (3301); Temple Bar (1728).

Adding further evidence of the overwhelming influence of Freemasonry is the list of some 6000 of the nation's most prominent Masons, filling 122 pages of the *Masonic Yearbook*: eminent lawyers, industrialists, merchant bankers, local councillors, academics, doctors, assistant chief constables, churchmen, MPs, HM Inspectors of Constabulary, high-ranking officers of the armed forces, knights, lords and baronets.

The *Yearbook* also provides detailed information on the organization's regional bureaucracy. The 1988/89 edition shows, for example, that Kent is divided into two areas – East and West. The Grand Superintendent of the East Kent Provincial Grand Chapter, the most senior Freemason in East Kent, is shown as Brien C. Stigant who has held that position since 1985. Mr Stigant is a senior partner in the Chatham firm of solicitors, Redfern and Stigant, in the area.

The second most senior officer in the East Kent area is Provincial Grand Master John A. Porter TD, JP, DL. According to his entry in *Who's Who* Mr Porter is a prominent local estate agent, a director of numerous building societies, has a military background, was president of the Gravesend Conservative Association from 1965 until 1977, has been a magistrate since 1952, a commissioner of taxes since 1970 and is a former president of Kent County Cricket Club. A true establishment man.

The same can indeed be said of the Grand Superintendent of the West Kent Provincial Grand Chapter, who also holds office as West Kent's Provincial Grand Master, Simon F. N. Waley QC. Better known as His Honour Judge Felix Waley QC, he is a very powerful figure – Charterhouse, Oxford, the Royal Navy, Middle Temple barrister, Court Recorder, Crown Court Judge and former Conservative councillor and parliamentary candidate.

A closer examination of the Masonic lodges in the Medway towns of Rochester, Chatham and Gillingham – the commercial hub of Kent – shows just how much of a powerhouse a local Masonic fraternity can be. At least four lodges – King's Navy (lodge no. 2901), White Ensign of Gillingham (4180), Royal Engineers Chatham (4465) and General Gordon (4292) – are directly connected to the armed forces, particularly the Navy. The local council has also two lodges in the area, as does the police.

The Medway towns telephone directory lists three Masonic clubs: the Chatham & District Freemasons Hall & Club Ltd; the Gillingham Masonic Club & Co. Ltd; and the Rochester Masonic Hall & Club Ltd. Each club is a limited company so a complete set of accounts is available from Companies House (*see* pp. 16–17). These give a detailed insight into the local Masonic network. All directors of the clubs are listed together with their addresses, occupations and details of any other directorships. The names of shareholders – usually the more influential of the local masonic lodges – are also given.

Apart from local Masonic clubs and halls, many of the national Masonic organizations are also limited companies, such as the Royal Masonic Benevolent Institution (RMBI Services Ltd and RMBI Nominees Ltd), and the Central London Masonic Centre Ltd (euphemistically listed in the telephone directory as the London Masonic Centre).

The *Data Protection Register* (*DPR*) is also a source of information on a number of key Masonic organizations: Supreme Grand Chapter of Royal Arch Masons of England (*DPR* no. AO835175); United Grand Lodge of England (AO835158); Staff Pension and Life Assurances Scheme of the Grand Lodge (A0835189); Grand Charity of the United Grand Lodge of England (A0835161); Royal Masonic Benevolent Institution (D0095204);

Masonic Province of West Kent (B0800026); Trustees of the Royal Masonic Hospital (C0388069).

MASONIC CHECKLIST

Although it is a secretive organization, much information is available on Freemasonry from such sources as:

- *The Masonic Yearbook*
- Companies House records
- The *Data Protection Register*
- Charities index
- press coverage

Further detailed information on the subject in the public domain includes *The Brotherhood* by Stephen Knight and *Inside the Brotherhood* by Martin Short (both published by Grafton). A slightly more obscure publication, *The Secret Society of the Freemasons in Bradford: an investigation* (£3.00, 1 in 12 Publications, 31 Manor Row, Bradford 1), is an excellent example of how information on this subject can be pulled together from the sources outlined above and from local media reports, forming a detailed study of the influence of local Freemasons in one particular area.

One of the more pernicious aspects of the Masonic fraternity, however, is the way that a local network of Freemasons can ruin anyone who stands in its way. One Freemason interviewed by Stephen Knight explained that Freemasonry's nationwide organization of men from most walks of life provides one of the most efficient private intelligence networks imaginable – no need for a Freedom of Information Act for them! Private information on anyone in the country can normally be accessed very rapidly through endless permutations of Masonic contacts – police, magistrates, solicitors, bank managers, Post Office staff ('very useful in supplying copies of a man's mail'), doctors, government employees, bosses of firms and nationalized industries and so on.

So, by combining information from yearbooks, the local telephone directory, Companies House records, the *Data Protection Register*, other existing published sources and local press cuttings, it is possible to start building up a detailed study of local networks and prominent local individuals. By also combing local reference library files and by talking to people involved, it is possible to conduct very detailed research into any organization. Local reference libraries keep files on local clubs and societies, and these should be thoroughly examined to see who wields the power. In particular, check details of Rotary Clubs and Round Tables as they are often said to be linked to Freemasonry. They are certainly a meeting place of the self-appointed local élite.

Despite the complexities of researching voluntary organizations, there are a number of useful directories in this area:

- *Councils, Committees and Boards.* This handbook lists thousands of advisory, consultative, executive and voluntary bodies in British public life, from the Aberdeen & District Milk Marketing Board to the Youth Committee for Northern Ireland. The book is arranged in four sections: alphabetical directory; index to acronyms and abbreviated names; index to chairmen; subject index of activities and fields of interest. It lists details of each organization including: name; address; date of establishment; composition of membership; names of chairman and secretary; terms of reference; activities.

- *Directory of British Associations.* This locates and identifies over 8000 national societies and associations – and certain categories of regional and local organizations – in many fields of interest and activity, including: trade associations; professional institutes; learned societies; chambers of commerce; trade unions; religious groups; political organizations; quangos.

- *Centres and Bureaux.* This is a new directory that identifies con-centrations of effort, information and expertise, from the Advisory Centre for Education to the Women's Reproductive Rights Infor-mation Centre. Entries include: address details; names of principal staff; when and by whom established; how financed; objects; acti-vities and services to the public; publications.

- *The Voluntary Agencies Directory.* More than 2000 of Britain's leading voluntary agencies are listed in this directory, which is the standard reference work in its field. The organizations included range from small, specialist self-help groups to long-established, national charities. Company names are included, where appro-priate.

The first three directories are published by CBD Research Publications. *The Voluntary Agencies Directory* is published by the Bedford Square Press.

VOLUNTARY GROUPS CHECKLIST
Information available on local groups may include:

- files in the local reference library
- coverage by the local press

- listings in the *Directory of British Associations*
- local charities index
- Companies House index and records

Charities

More than 161,000 charities are registered in the UK and, between them, attract over £15 billion in donations and grants each year – the equivalent of approximately 3 per cent of the gross national product (GNP). The majority of charities, which are regulated by the Charities Act, 1960, are bona fide organizations. But some – such as quasi-political groups and some religious organizations – engage in controversial activities that the researcher may wish to examine in some detail.

Any organization that calls itself a charity will be registered either with the Charity Commission or the Registrar of Friendly Societies or will be a company limited by guarantee (*see* Friendly Societies, p. 72; Companies, pp. 16–17). When investigating a charity, it is always worthwhile checking its name against the Companies House index as many charities are also limited companies.

The Charity Commission maintains files on every charity and these are open for public inspection. Each file contains a 'governing document', such as a trust deed or constitution; the charity's original application to register as a charity; and copies of recent accounts. These documents should reveal the charity's policies, sources of funding, projects undertaken and the names of the people on the board of management. There is no search fee for inspecting a file, but the Charity Commission advises inquirers to phone first so that the appropriate file can be located and made readily available for inspection. Photocopies may be taken at a nominal fee, and the Commission is prepared to deal with inquiries by post.

CHARITIES CHECKLIST
Information on charities can be found in a number of places:

- local Charities index
- *The Charities Digest*
- Charity Commission's files
- Registry of Friendly Societies
- Companies House

The Charity Commission also maintains local indexes of charities around the country. Each county council keeps an up-to-date index, supplied by the Commission, of all charities in their area, as do most district and borough councils. These indexes give less detailed information than that held on the Commission's main files, but provide a useful starting point for any inquiry. Contact your local library or town hall for further information.

The Charity Commissioners publish 36 free explanatory leaflets on their work and charity law. Leaflet CC9, for example, is entitled *Political Activities by Charities*, and CC29 covers *Charities and Local Authorities*. A list of all their leaflets is available from the Commission.

A number of directories is published on charities in addition to the above mentioned *Voluntary Agencies Directory*:

- *The Charities Digest*. Published by the Charities Aid Foundation, this is the principal reference book on the subject and provides information on over 1200 charities in the UK. It also gives details of the work of the Charity Commission, the Central Register and the Official Custodian and provides an outline of charity law, registration and regulation.

- *The Directory of Grant-Making Trusts*. Published by the Charities Aid Foundation, this 'encyclopaedia of treasure-houses' lists around 3000 grant-making trusts, ranging from major household names, such as Rowntree and the Wellcome Trust, to local trusts with only a few thousand pounds in annual awards. Cross-referenced in various categories (e.g. international, sciences, humanities, education, welfare), each entry lists: year of establishment; objects and policy; restrictions; financial status.

- *A Guide to the Major Trusts*. Published by the Directory of Social Change, this lists the UK's top 430 trusts in terms of financial size, from the Wellcome Trust (£38,500,000 per annum) to the Grundy Foundation (£17,000 per annum). A useful appendix lists, by county, agencies that advise voluntary groups and charities.

- *A Guide to Company Giving*. This guide, published by the Directory of Social Change, surveys the top 300 companies in the donations stakes, with chapters on: tax and company giving; how to do an appeal; company trusts; sponsorship; local enterprise agencies; payroll giving. However, it avoids the thorny issue of donations to political parties and causes.

Friendly societies

Friendly societies include more than 10,000 non-profit-making bodies with limited liability, such as building societies, cooperatives, housing associations and companies registered under the Industrial and Provident Societies Acts – working men's clubs, savings societies and the like. They are required to file documents and annual returns with the Registry of Friendly Societies.

The files at the Registry are available for inspection and show such details as the names and addresses of directors, latest annual return and accounts, membership, shareholders and registered office. The file on each friendly society costs £3.20 to inspect, and photocopies are charged at 15p per page. There is no facility for postal searches and the Registry requires a minimum of three hours' notice for the files to be located. However, many friendly societies are also companies limited by guarantee, and detailed information will therefore be available from Companies House (*see* pp. 16–17). So the Companies House Index, as well as other sources of business information, should be checked before trekking off to the Registry of Friendly Societies in London's West End.

Churches and religious organizations

These are still very powerful forces in our society, and control multi-million pound budgets and huge property portfolios. They play an active part in the affairs of State, and many are extremely influential at a local level.

Despite their esoteric nature, religious organizations are very down-to-earth when it comes to their business activities. Many churches also operate as limited companies, charities, friendly societies and housing associations – which means that a mass of information is available to the researcher interested in their activities. For example, the Church Commissioners of the Church of England own a number of property holding companies, including Church Estates Development and Improvement Co. Ltd and Elmswood Ltd, to hold and manage their huge £1.36 billion property portfolio.

However, it's not only the traditional churches that engage in such commercial business activities. The Worldwide Church of God, the Pasadena-based publisher of *The Plain Truth* (of which more than 7 million free copies are distributed worldwide each month), is both a limited company and a registered charity in the UK. It has two subsidiaries – Ambassador Press Ltd and Ambassador College (UK) Ltd – the latter operating a mainframe computer system which is registered on the *Data Protection Register* and listed in the *Computer Users' Yearbook*. Therefore, when conducting this type of research, religious organizations have to be viewed in the same way as commercial organizations or other voluntary bodies.

Most religions publish a yearbook detailing their activities, and the main ones are:

- *Baptist Union Directory*
- *Buddhist Directory*
- *Catholic Directory*
- *Church of England Yearbook*
- *Church of Scotland Yearbook*
- *Crockford's Clerical Directory* (a *Who's Who* of the Church of England)
- *Fellowship of Independent Evangelical Churches Yearbook*
- *Friends' Book of Meeting Yearbook* (Quakers)
- *Garlick's Methodist Directory*
- *General Assembly of Unitarian and Free Churches Directory*
- *The Good Churches Guide*
- *Jewish Yearbook*
- *Salvation Army Yearbook*
- *United Reformed Church Yearbook*
- *Zionist Yearbook*

6 LAW AND ORDER

Although this chapter deals primarily with those law and order agencies that the public comes into contact with on a regular basis, such as the police and the probation service, some of the more obscure areas of law enforcement are also covered, including the armed forces and the security services.

The availability of information on agencies in these different categories is extremely fickle. That was certainly the conclusion of civil rights activists in Kent who, in 1982, became aware that the local constabulary was planning to buy a £1.5 million mainframe computer. A request for information about the uses to which the computer would be put was instantly rejected by the Chief Constable who refused to disclose any details about the project. Two weeks later, the police advertised in a local newspaper for a manager to run the Kent police computer. Simply by sending off for a job description and application form under a *nom de plume*, the activists were able to obtain a copy of the 'detailed operational specification' of the computer – much to the embarrassment of the Kent Constabulary once this simple research technique was revealed in the local press.

Significantly, though, this information would now be available under the Local Government (Access to Information) Act, as the Kent Police Authority is a sub-committee of Kent County Council. And a considerable amount of detailed information has to be published on all police computers in the *Data Protection Register* as required by the 1984 Data Protection Act. Nevertheless this case proves that a little lateral thinking is needed in any research project.

For instance, the entry for the Police National Computer on the *Data Protection Register* reveals that the police obtain information about suspects from a vast range of sources: Customs and Excise, the Driver and Vehicle

Licensing Centre, the Departments of Health and Social Security, the Home Office, the Ministry of Defence (including the armed forces), local authority social services departments, banks, insurance companies, lawyers, public libraries, press and media, the Post Office Investigation Department, victim support groups and so on. And according to the Police National Computer itself, the following types of information is held on offenders: personal details, habits, personality, character, possessions, movement details, ethnic origin, criminal intelligence, uncategorized information.

Other right-to-know laws can be used, too. Members of a community newspaper in Manchester were able to find out that the local constabulary possessed sub-machine guns by using section 228 of the Local Government Act, 1972. By demanding (as was their right) that the local police authority show them the 'orders for the payment of money', they saw documents that confirmed the purchase of the guns.

But just because a legal right for access to information exists does not mean that the public will actually be able to obtain that information. For example, it is the policy of the Lord Chancellor's Department that a list of the names of Justices of the Peace (JPs or magistrates) serving each area should be available for inspection at each magistrates' court. This was backed up in 1986 by the case of *Regina v Felixstowe Magistrates' Court ex parte Leigh and the Observer Ltd*, in which the High Court ruled that the press and the public have a right to know the names of their magistrates. However, a survey of the 14 magistrates' courts in inner London carried out by members of the National Council for Civil Liberties in March 1987 revealed that none of those courts would provide the lists of magistrates as required by the Lord Chancellor's Department. This is an example where, because of the obsessive secrecy, it is entirely justifiable to enlist the services of the press in order to draw public attention to the problem.

The contentious issue of the security services is also dealt with briefly in this chapter. As outlined in the introduction, there is a considerable amount of myth about the work and nature of spies, as the case of the 1988 Farnborough Air Show demonstrated. Ministry of Defence police were called in to investigate a break-in when it was discovered that a spy had entered the McDonnell Douglas display area at night. A helmet had been taken apart and an intricate arrangement of lenses – which enables a fighter pilot to shoot at a target even though it might be flying at right angles to his missiles – had been photographed. This spying mission could have been fulfilled quite legally; the patent for the helmet and detailed diagrams of it are quite freely available for inspection at the British Library!

The police

As the Kent police computer case points out, the local police authorities are sub-committees of the county council – outside of the Metropolitan Police area – and thus subject to the right-to-know provisions in local government law. This gives the public the right to attend meetings of the police authority and those of any sub-committees that it might set up, and the right to inspect background documents. More detailed information can be obtained by pursuing section 228 of the Local Government Act, 1972, and at the time of audit when any member of the public has the right to 'inspect the accounts to be audited and all books, deeds, contracts, bills, vouchers and receipts . . .' (*See* Chapter 3 for details of these rights-to-know.) Police officers are, therefore, local government officers whose duties are regulated by specific pieces of legislation – just like other town hall employees.

POLICE CHECKLIST
The main sources of information on the police are:

- *Police and Constabulary Almanac*
- the Chief Constable's Annual Report
- minutes of local police committee meetings
- the *Data Protection Register*
- press cuttings

Another source of information on the local constabulary will be the local press. Some local and regional newspapers make their own libraries available for use by residents conducting detailed research, although the main local reference libraries should have some sort of press cuttings files.

The principal reference book on the police in the UK is the *Police and Constabulary Almanac*, published by Hazell. It provides detailed information on every constabulary in the UK including the Royal Parks Constabulary, Royal Botanic Gardens Constabulary, Ministry of Defence Police, British Transport Police, UK Atomic Energy Authority Constabulary, RAF Police, Corps of Royal Military Police, Royal Marines Police, Royal Naval Regulatory Branch (Naval Provost) – as well as each county constabulary.

The *Almanac* also includes details on the Home Office Police Department, including the C5 Division Drugs Branch, Scientific Research and Development Branch, Police Requirement Support Unit, Central Planning Units, Police National Computer Organization, Forensic Science Service, HM Inspectors of Constabulary, Police Training Centres. In addition, the Association of Chief Police Officers (ACPO), the Superintendents' Association and the Police Federation are detailed in the *Almanac*, as are the various regional criminal squads and the police services in the Isle of Man, the Channel Islands and the Republic of Ireland. The book even covers the police arrangements at each port, harbour, dock, tunnel and airport as well as the policing role of such organizations as the Post Office Investigation Department, BBC Investigator's Office, Customs and Excise and so on.

Complaints against the police are investigated by the Police Complaints Authority, but this body has made a complaint of its own – that the law sometimes requires it to be excessively secretive about the cases it investigates. Section 98 of the Police and Criminal Evidence Act, 1984, makes it an offence for a member of the Authority to identify publicly anyone involved in its investigations. The Authority's chairman, Sir Cecil Clothier, has pointed out that, while anonymity is generally necessary, there are exceptions. 'Sometimes the case is so notorious that the whole world knows who is involved,' he said. He has called for the law to be changed to give the Authority discretion to publish information that would be in the public interest to disclose, subject to the needs of confidentiality.

Legal professions

A number of directories and yearbooks provide information on the legal professions and their various organizations:

- *The Solicitors and Barristers Directory*, published by Waterlow Publishers, is by far the most comprehensive of the legal directories. It lists: every individual solicitor and firm; every barrister in private practice and each set of chambers in England and Wales; law costs draftsmen; legal executives; barristers' clerks; international lawyers; government law officers; Treasury counsel; judges; recorders; registrars; stipendiary (full-time salaried) magistrates; coroners; and high sheriffs. The directory provides a detailed analysis of the Law Society (including the Legal Aid Board), the Bar Council, Solicitor Complaints Bureau, College of Law, Barristers' Clerks Association and so on. All civil and criminal courts in England and Wales are listed, as are the various legal tribunals.

- The *Butterworth Law Directory*, published by Butterworth, is a less thorough guide to the profession, but nevertheless adequate for most purposes. The *Scottish Law Directory* details the Scottish legal system, including the courts, court officers, law officers, solicitors, advocates and useful facts and figures on the system there. For

Northern Ireland, the *Law Directory* is published by the Incorporated Law Society of Ireland and includes a register of all solicitors in Ulster.

- For more detailed information on the work undertaken by individual firms of solicitors, the *Solicitors Regional Directory* published annually by the Law Society is useful. A guide entitled *The Legal 500: the major law firms in England, Wales and Scotland*, published by Legaleast, analyses in some detail the categories of work undertaken by the top 500 law firms.

- *Kimes International Law Directory*, published by Kimes, lists legal practices in most principal towns throughout the world. The International Law List provides details of law practices in some 153 countries worldwide that are associated with British solicitors or who have British-trained solicitors or barristers on their staff.

- *NAPO Probation Directory*, published by Wells, lists every probation office in the country and senior probation personnel. It also provides a comprehensive guide to the prisons, hostels and other penal institutions in the UK, and many penal reform groups and campaigning organizations.

- A number of guides provide information on the wide range of para-legal services including private detectives, inquiry agencies, debt collectors, process servers, law agents. The main publication in this field, produced by Regency International Publications, is *The Regency International Directory* which, as its name suggests, gives an international view of the business. Alternatively *Butterworth's Legal Services Directory*, published by British Media Publications, provides a thorough guide to the para-legal professions: and also covers arbitrators, expert witnesses, translators, loss adjusters, parliamentary agents, patent and trademark agents, photographers, security equipment and services, shorthand writers, etc.

It should be noted that the sometimes murky world of the private detective or inquiry agent is completely unregulated, and anyone can set themselves up without the need to register with a professional or official body. Some organizations in the private security field – Control Risks, KMS, Zeus Security Consultants and Defence Systems – have been associated with the security services and, it has been suggested, some of them with such activities as the supply of mercenaries. The bigger detective agencies and security service companies, however, tend to be registered at Companies House as limited companies, as well as under the Data Protection Act.

The armed forces and diplomats

Relatively little information is available on the armed forces. There are, however, one or two sources that are in the public domain and which can provide a surprisingly candid insight into the armed forces:

- *Jane's Information Group.* This company publishes a mass of information on defence matters, and describes itself as 'the leading international defence and aerospace information provider, and a major supplier of data to clients from industry and government worldwide'. Products and services offered include: daily and weekly newsletters, weekly and monthly magazines, Jane's year-books, DMS market intelligence reports, market studies, forecasts, books and electronic databases.

   But at a price. For example, the DMS market intelligence report on 'Command, Control, Communications & Intelligence' comes with a £700 price tag. The *International Defense Newsletter* costs £165 for a year's subscription, whereas *Jane's Security and CO-IN Equipment 1989–90* ('The 2nd edition gives you complete information on the equipment used by military, paramilitary and security forces in internal security and counter-insurgency operations') seems a snip at only £65. However, some of the more important revelations contained in the Jane's series do make the news pages of the quality press. In April 1988 the *Guardian* published a report on a Soviet innovation in deep-sea radio communications for sub-marines that appeared in the 1988 edition of *Jane's Military Communications* (£95).

   Few public libraries stock Jane's publications; the British Library Business Information Service stocks *Jane's Defence Weekly* ('the authoritative tri-service defence weekly covering the latest military developments, personnel changes, business news, intelligence, and the latest contracts' – £72 p.a.). Jane's books published in the UK should be available for inspection in the British Library Reading Room for which a pass is required (*see* p. 113). Jane's catalogue is available free from: Jane's Information Group, Sentinel House, 163 Brighton Rd, Coulston, Surrey CR3 2NX, tel. (081) 763 1030.

- *The Military Balance* (published by the International Institute of Strategic Studies) is a highly detailed analysis of the military capability of each Warsaw Pact and NATO country – for example, the 1988–89 edition states that the British Army currently has 870 Chieftain tanks in service.

- *The British Defence Directory* is a quarterly periodical published by Brassey's – a division of the Maxwell Pergamon Publishing Corporation – for £210 annually (or £52.50 per edition). It describes itself as 'the quarterly, computerized, regularly updated directory of senior service and civilian personnel in the Ministry of Defence, Royal Navy, Army, Royal Air Force and NATO, and in-service diplomatic posts – comprehensively indexed'. It is indeed a very detailed *Who's Who* in the defence field although it stops short of giving away any secrets. For example, in the section on Chief of Defence Intelligence, the names of the various heads of department are left blank, although the direct phone lines are given. It lists by country the various 'defence liaison staff' at the Ministry of Defence, plus the foreign service attachés at the various embassies in London and the UK service attachés in our embassies abroad, and the senior personnel in the Ministry of Defence's commercial arm, International Military Services Ltd.

  Brassey's also publishes a wide range of books and journals on international relations and military affairs. A catalogue is available from them at 24 Gray's Inn Rd, London WC1X 8HR.

- On the subject of military personnel, definitive lists of senior service personnel are published each year by HMSO: *The Air Force List*, *The RAF Retired List*, *The Navy List* and *The Army List*.

- A number of publications are available on the diplomatic side of the defence industry: *The Diplomatic Service List* (HMSO) is a list of our diplomats abroad. The *London Diplomatic List* details the diplomatic staff in attendance at the various embassies in London. Another, and more thorough, source of information about foreign diplomats in London is in the *Diplomatic and Consular Yearbook* (HMSO).

- A number of peace groups and campaigning organizations, such as the Campaign Against the Arms Trade and the Peace Pledge Union, provide information on defence matters through their libraries and publications. *Peace & Security: a guide to individual groups and grant sources* is a comprehensive guide to such groups in the UK, published by the Directory of Social Change. Another is *Peace Movements of the World*, published by Croom Helm, which provides a country-by-country guide to peace groups.

ARMED FORCES AND DIPLOMATS CHECKLIST

Little information is available on the armed forces apart from that published in books and newspapers. The main sources are:

- Jane's publications
- *British Defence Directory*
- *The Military Balance*
- *Diplomatic Service List*
- *Diplomatic and Consular Yearbook*

Spies and spying

As the introduction pointed out, this book is not for conspiracy theorists but for individuals and groups who wish to find out a little more about the institutions in our society that exercise power over their lives. Although few of us will ever have any dealings with the security services or their agents, it has been established that MI5 and the police Special Branch take an active interest in such 'subversives' as peace campaigners, trade unionists and civil rights activists; indeed, it is estimated that the Special Branch nationally has files on some 2 million citizens. The security services may, therefore, at some time receive the attention of the active citizen. However, if you are an historian you may find your research impeded by the secret services. In November 1977, *The Times* revealed that government papers on the setting up of the new state of Israel following World War II will not be available for public inspection until the year 2022 – simply because they mention the existence of MI6 which is not officially acknowledged to exist in peacetime.

The most detailed single source on the workings of the security services MI5 and MI6, as well as the Special Branch and military intelligence, is an obscure magazine called *Lobster*. Set up in 1983 by two researchers, Robin Ramsey and Steve Dorril, *Lobster* has covered a wide range of issues involving the security services. Recent issues have covered: counter-insurgency and dirty tricks in Northern Ireland; MI5 plots to smear British politicians; the death of Hilda Murrell; Ken Livingstone's questions about the use of black propaganda and misinformation by the security services in Northern Ireland; Kim Philby's disclosures; the London CIA station; anti-Labour forgeries; and similar topics. In May 1989, *Lobster* published a *Who's Who in the British Secret State* (Lobster Special, £5.00) which chronicles the careers of hundreds of suspected and confirmed British intelligence officers. *Lobster* did this by scouring the pages of books on the intelligence services by such distinguished authors as Chapman Pincher, Nigel West (aka Rupert

Allason MP), Anthony Cavendish and David Leigh and compiling bio-
graphies on all the intelligence officers named. *Lobster* points out that the
information they have gleaned is not conclusive evidence by itself, and
should only be used as a starting point for further research. *Lobster* appears
only occasionally – three times during 1989 – and a subscription costs £4.00.
Back copies are available for issues 9 to 17; a complete set will cost you
£16.75. *Lobster*'s address is: 214 Westbourne Ave, Hull HU5 3JB.

An international database of intelligence matters and personnel, *Spy-
BASE*, is available from Micro Associates, PO Box 5369, Arlington, VA
22205, USA and costs $45. *SpyBASE* contains over 66,000 citations collated
from hundreds of published sources – including *Lobster*. The data base is
compatible with a number of computer systems such as IBM and Macintosh.
Details are available from Micro Associates.

The use of limited companies by almost every type of organization has
been highlighted throughout this book, and the security services are not
totally exempt from registration at Companies House. For instance, the
Secret Intelligence Service, MI6, runs a pension fund for its staff and
associates – Century Benevolent Fund Ltd, and there may well be other
registered companies operated by the security services.

A mass of information has been published in this country on intelligence
matters – in books, newspapers and magazines. Recent changes in the
Official Secrets Act may slow down the flow of this, but previously published
information will continue to be available through public reference libraries.
For example, on 6 April 1988 the *Guardian* published a full-page supplement
on the various security services, with flow-charts of their internal structures,
the names of senior personnel and the addresses of their various offices. The
security services have also been extensively documented by the *New Statesman* (now *New Statesman and Society*) magazine, which in 1981 published
a booklet on the subject called *Big Brother is Listening*, which includes a
chapter entitled 'Big Brother's Many Mansions'. Few people will need – or
be in a position – to conduct their own primary research into this subject, so
use existing reference sources (*see* Press cuttings, p. 88).

The interception of communications tribunal

In 1985, the Interception of Communications Tribunal came into existence
following a number of embarrassing revelations when the tapping of tele-
phones by British government agencies were found by the European Court
of Human Rights to be in breach of the right to privacy. The ICT makes little
information about its work available to the public, but in a written answer to

an MP's question in May 1987, the Home Secretary reported: 'There have been 41 applications for a tribunal investigation under Section 7(2) of the Interception of Communications Act, 1985 during the period of 10 April 1986 to 9 April 1987. Investigation of 36 applications has been completed: on no occasion has the tribunal concluded that there has been a contravention of Sections 2 to 5 of the Act.' Consequently the National Council for Civil Liberties described the Interception of Communication Act, 1985 as 'a snooper's charter'.

- The NCCL publishes an 'NCCL Briefing', *The Interception of Communications*, which comments on the Act in some considerable detail. It is available for £2.00 from the NCCL.
- The Interception of Communications Tribunal publishes a leaflet on the workings of the Act which is available from the Interception of Communications Tribunal, PO Box 44, St Christopher House, 80–112 Southwark St, London SE1 0XT, tel. (071) 921 1277.

7 INVESTIGATING AND USING THE MEDIA

Newspapers, magazines, radio stations and television networks are clearly very powerful institutions in any society – and that is certainly the case in the United Kingdom in the 1990s. Such institutions provide detailed coverage of the many day-to-day events that directly affect our lives. But some fail to cover certain contentious issues – particularly at a local level – such as local government corruption or Freemasonry. This is not necessarily through wilful neglect; it can be due to the laziness of reporters or the failure of their newspapers to invest in investigative journalism.

However, because of their inherent power, newspapers and broadcasting companies may well be the subject of the researcher's attention, not least to find out who owns and works for them. Most newspapers and broadcast organizations (excluding the British Broadcasting Corporation) are companies, and so information can be obtained from Companies House and published business information sources in the same way as for any other company.

In addition, the 'products' of the media, especially newspapers, are also key sources of information on all aspects of life. Press cuttings are particularly useful, and should be checked when conducting investigative research on business executives, companies, political groups, official bodies and the like.

Investigating the media

A substantial amount of information is regularly published on media organizations, their audiences and their output. Most depend on advertising revenue for their existence, and this means that large quantities of market research data are also available. The main sources of information are:

- *Benn's Media Directory* (published by Benn's Business Information Services, 2 vols, £65.00 for both). This is the most substantial guide to the media in the UK and covers almost every local and national newspaper, periodical, radio station and TV broadcast company. It details basic information about each company (including a comprehensive list of directors and senior executive staff) plus: classified index of local newspapers by county; local newspapers in detail; classified index of periodicals and free magazines; media directories and other reference serials; classified index of agencies and services to the media industry; details of all BBC and independent broadcasting organizations.

- *Willing's Press Guide* (published by British Media Publications, £54.00). This lists over ll,000 of the UK's daily, Sunday, county and local newspapers, periodicals and annuals. The guide provides details of: frequency of publication; address; cover price; circulation figures; editor; advertising director; circulation director; publisher/holding company; and covers key overseas newspapers and periodicals as well. It has a number of indexes, including: classified index; a town-by-town guide of local newspapers in the UK and Ireland; and an alphabetical list of magazine and periodical publishers and their titles.

- *Writers' and Artists' Yearbook* (published by A & C Black, £6.95). A very useful paperback that provides basic information on UK newspapers and magazines; book publishers; literary agents; broadcasting organizations; syndicates, news and press agencies. A must for anyone seriously engaged in the business of writing.

- *BRAD* (published by British Rate and Data and is available on subscription). This stands for 'British Rates and Data' and is a detailed monthly guide to all advertising media. It provides facts and figures on the advertising rates for newspapers, business journals, consumer publications, and independent TV and radio stations. For example, at the end of 1989 it would have cost £14,000 to take out a full-page advertisement in the *Guardian* but only £408 in the *Hinckley Times*. *BRAD* is a very useful way of calculating the economics of a particular newspaper or broadcasting company, and those who advertise in them. It can also be used simply to find out the titles of specialist magazines.

- *Blue Book of British Broadcasting* (published by Tellex Monitors, £21.00). This is the main directory on the BBC and independent broadcasting organizations in the UK. It has sections on BBC news and current affairs; BBC television; BBC radio; BBC educational broadcasting; BBC regional broadcasting, including local radio; the Independent Broadcasting Authority; independent television companies; commercial radio; cable and satellite broadcasting. The Blue Book outlines the services provided by the broadcasting authorities and companies and includes a who's who of directors and senior personnel.

- *Kemp's International Film and Television Yearbook* (published by Kemp's, £28.00). This contains over 1600 pages of detailed information on the film and television industries and related services from animation equipment to voice-overs, and includes television production companies, the trade press and trade and professional associations.

- *The Film and Television Yearbook* (published by the British Film Institute, £10.95). Published by the British Film Institute and details the huge resources of the film and television businesses, including: archives and libraries; cinemas; courses; government involvement; press contacts; trade organizations.

- *Advertisers' Annual* (published by Skinner, £49.00). This is the main reference book on the advertising and allied industries, and now comes in three volumes. Volume 1 contains extensive information on over 2500 advertising agencies, public relations companies, sales promotion consultants, sponsorship consultants and recruitment agencies. It also lists over 17,000 advertisers and their respective agencies. Volume 2 gives details of the media throughout the world, divided into 'The UK' and 'Overseas', and provides information on newspapers, periodicals, TV, radio, cinema, transport advertising, and outdoor and poster companies. Volume 3 lists over 7000 firms servicing the marketing and advertising industries such as artists, conference organizers, copywriters, desk-top publishing outfits, research services.

- *Hollis Press and Public Relations Manual* (published by Hollis Directories, £35.50). This comprises more than 1240 pages in five sections covering: news contacts in the commercial, industrial, consumer, professional, financial and corporate sectors; official and public information sources; public relations consultancies (including a regional guide); reference and research sources; services and supplies. The manual also includes (in Section 4) a directory of 'parliamentary consultants' – that is, commercial organizations that provide professional political lobbying to anybody who is able to pay for such services.

- *The Creative Handbook* (published by British Media Publications, £40.00). This is a detailed guide to the 'creative' industries, and includes information on suppliers of photographic services, film and video, advertising, print, design and graphics, etc.

- *Directory of Publishing* (published by Cassell and the Publishers Association, £26.00). This detailed directory lists more than 1100 publishers from 23 countries, plus literary agents, packagers, distributors, book clubs and a variety of trade and allied services.

- *Directory of Book Publishers and Wholesalers* (published by the Booksellers Association, £30.00). This directory is compiled and published by the Booksellers Association, and lists all but the most obscure publishers in the UK. Details each publisher and lists their directors and senior executives and outlines their areas of publishing.

- *5001 Hard-to-Find Publishers and Their Addresses* (published by Allan Armstrong and Associates). Despite its self-explanatory title, the third edition of this directory actually lists over 7500 publishers and their addresses and telephone numbers.

- *Using the Media: how to deal with the press, television and radio* (published by Pluto, now out of print). This guide by Denis MacShane on how to obtain coverage in the press and on radio and television is the most useful handbook available for anyone wishing to intervene more effectively in the production of news. Although the second edition was published as long ago as in 1983, it still contains a mass of helpful advice and information for community activists. Copies should still be available at libraries and advice centres.

- Campaign for Press and Broadcasting Freedom (CPBF). This organization campaigns against media censorship, for more public access and a right of reply. The CPBF can be contacted at 9 Poland St, London W1V 3DG, tel. (071) 437 2795.

- National Union of Journalists. The NUJ maintains inside expert knowledge of media organizations and publishes a range of literature on the subject. It can be contacted at Acorn House, 314 Gray's Inn Rd, London WC1X 8DP, tel. (071) 278 7916.

Press cuttings: using the media

" A good test of democracy is that there should be a presupposition in favour of openness, not a presupposition in favour of secrecy. In Britain, it is the other way round – a principle now enshrined in this new legislation. Instead of reforming Section 2 [of the Official Secrets Act], we should have abolished it altogether and replaced it with a Freedom of Information Act, bringing this country into line with most Western democracies.

Donald Trelford in the *Observer*

The press can be one of the most useful sources of information for any detailed research on just about any subject. Each year, millions of news stories and features on every conceivable subject are published in thousands of newspapers and magazines. But how can those stories be located? Fortunately a number of indexes are published giving details of most news and feature stories that have appeared the British press.

- *Clover Newspaper Index*. This covers a broad range of topics, issues and events reported in the national quality newspapers. The *Index* takes the form of an extremely detailed weekly bulletin, and is collected in looseleaf files. It is a very useful starting point for conducting background research on individuals and organizations.
- *Research Index*. This bulky publication provides an index of the news stories, primarily on business and financial subjects, that have appeared in the national newspapers and in over 100 trade and business periodicals. However, it is not limited to business information as its headings include: government departments; local government; politics; property; security services; trade unions; and newspapers and publishing.

  Each entry provides the title of the article, the name, date and page of the source publication; and the name of the company or organization referred to. Articles can be searched by company name, title of industry or title of article. This is a cumulative index with bi-weekly updates of 5000 to 6000 entries per issue.
- *Humanities Index*. This is a very comprehensive index of a wide range of newspapers and periodicals, covering the arts, economics, history, philosophy, politics and society. Not to be underestimated despite its staid title.
- Newspaper indexes. *The Times* newspaper publishes an annual index of its content, together with monthly updates for the current

year, as does the *Financial Times*. The *Guardian* also publishes an index, and an annual index is available for the *Times Literary Supplement* in main reference libraries.

Back copies

Once the references have been found in these indexes, it will be necessary to obtain copies of the publications themselves. Reference libraries keep back copies of newspapers and magazines, but the period of coverage may only be in months rather than years. However, the *Guardian*, *Independent*, *Times* and *Financial Times* are available on microfilm (from which photo-copies can be taken), thus enabling libraries to stock many years of back copies.

The Newspaper Library

The British Library operates the Newspaper Library at Colindale in north London. This contains 600,000 volumes and parcels of newspapers, and over 220,000 reels of microfilm occupying around 18 miles of shelving. The collection consists mainly of daily and weekly newspapers and periodicals, including London newspapers and journals from 1801 onwards. The News-paper Library can supply photocopies of items from its newspaper collection provided that accurate references are supplied. This can be done via your local library service, by post or by visiting the Newspaper Library in person.

Telephone inquiries about specific items can be made on (071) 636 1544 ext. 7676, or direct dial on (071) 323 7676. General inquiries can be made by telephoning (071) 636 1544 ext. 7353, or direct dial on (071) 323 7353. For photocopy inquiries, telephone (071) 636 1544 ext. 7355, or direct dial (071) 323 7355. The address is: The British Library Newspaper Library, Colindale Avenue, London NW9 5HE. It is located directly opposite Colin-dale tube station, and is open Monday to Saturday, from 10.00 am to 5.00 pm.

Local newspapers

There is no index of the contents of local and provincial newspapers, but many reference libraries keep their own files of press cuttings on topics of local interest. These can include local government, businesses, personalities and events. The quantity and subject matter will vary from library to library, and anyone carrying out investigative research should certainly familiarize themselves with the press cuttings held in their local library. In addition, many local newspapers provide access to their back copies.

Telephone services

The Daily Telegraph Information Service on (071) 538 5000 provides an information service to the public on most subjects – except for callers trying to answer crosswords or competitions.

8 THE POLITICAL ARENA

" Ostrich-like, determined to insulate Britain from the outside
world, the government pulled up the blanket higher, tucked it in
tighter, confirming the established view among Britain's puzzled
and closest allies that the obsession with secrecy is now *le vice
Anglais.*

Richard Norton-Taylor in the *Guardian*

The political arena is made up of the politicians, the peerage, civil servants,
political parties, lobbyists, trade unions and 'think tanks' that play a major
part in the decision-making processes of this country. No apologies are made
for labouring the point that, since Parliament and the other institutions are
extensively covered in the press, newspaper indexes should be the first port
of call in any detailed research. Also bear in mind that the quality newspapers
such as the *Guardian* and *Independent* give extensive and critical coverage
of the affairs of State.

The first task of any research into government business or the political
machinery is to identify which department or official body does what. There
are hundreds of government departments, agencies, quangos and committees
that probe into almost every area of our lives. The two main reference books
to consult are the *Civil Service Yearbook* and *Public Bodies*.

The *Civil Service Yearbook* lists every government department in considerable detail. For example, the section on the Ministry of Defence covers 35
pages and outlines the activities of each department, and includes the names
of the Ministers and key civil servants – even down to their telephone
extensions.

Public Bodies is an annual government publication that lists more than 1600 quangos – public bodies that advise the government on a wide range of subjects from nuclear safety to butterfly conservation. With a combined budget of over £10 billion each year and a total staff of more than 150,000, they are extremely influential organizations.

Members of Parliament

The UK's 650 MPs are well documented, and they all have an entry in *Who's Who*. The annual *Register of Members' Interests* gives details of MPs financial interests, such as company directorships, trade union sponsorship, free travel abroad, and so on. However, the *Register* is not entirely without fault. For example, the Conservative MP John Selwyn Gummer is a member of the General Synod of the Church of England – a very influential British institution – but that membership does not show up on the Register. Although this does not imply any breach of parliamentary privilege, it does demonstrate that the researcher should not rely on any one source of information for important details – verification is always needed. Fuller biographical details of MPs are published in *Dod's Parliamentary Companion* (*see* p. 93) and in election leaflets and publicity material. The reference library serving a particular MP's constituency will keep files of election material going back many years; they are well worth looking through.

MPS CHECKLIST
The main sources of information on MPs are:

*   *Who's Who*
*   *Dod's Parliamentary Companion*
*   *Register of Members' Interests*
*   national press coverage
*   local newspapers
*   local reference library files

The aristocracy

Debrett's Peerage and Baronetage is the complete who's who of all titled UK citizens and royalty. *Debrett's* includes details of hereditary lords and ladies, life peers, life peeresses, law lords, lords spiritual, the baronetage, the Royal family, hereditary peeresses and peers who are minors, clubs, table of general precedence, forms of address of persons with titles, etc.

ARISTOCRACY CHECKLIST
Information on the British aristocracy can be found in:

- *Debrett's Peerage and Baronetage*
- old copies of *Burke's Peerage*
- *Who's Who*
- *Dod's Parliamentary Companion*
- newspaper indexes

Parliamentary information

66 The right of access to information which is of legitimate concern to people, Parliament and press is too restricted, and this, combined with the general secrecy in which government is conducted, has caused much injustice, some corruption and many mistakes.

Royal Commission on the Press, 1977

Almost every word that is spoken in the chambers of the Houses of Parliament is recorded in *Hansard*. This bulky document is available in some reference libraries, but normally newspaper coverage should suffice. Much more condensed is the House of Commons *Weekly Information Bulletin*, which gives: an outline of the progress of legislation; membership and activities of select committees and standing committees; the publication of White Papers and Green Papers. A complimentary copy is available free of charge by phoning (071) 219 4272 – the number of the House of Commons Public Information Office, which can be consulted on any House of Commons business. The House of Lords information office can be reached on (071) 219 3107. Individual constituents can, of course, enlist the services of their MPs to obtain parliamentary information.

A number of parliamentary handbooks provide details of the working of the Houses of Parliament. *Dod's Parliamentary Companion* gives thorough biographical details of MPs and members of the House of Lords. It also provides background information on government offices, ministers, committees, etc. A smaller guide is the pocket-sized *Vacher's Parliamentary Companion* which briefly describes each MP; it is up-to-date as it is published quarterly. *The Times Guide to the House of Commons* is published after each general election and provides a statistical analysis of every political party and constituency. *Erskine May's Parliamentary Practice* is known as the bible of parliamentary procedure, and gives incredibly complex information on the subject. Much more manageable is *Lobbying: An Insider's Guide* by the former Labour MP for Battersea, Alf Dubbs; it is the best guide available on using Parliament as a lobbying tool.

PARLIAMENTARY CHECKLIST

The proceedings of Parliament can be found in:

- national newspapers
- radio and television current affairs programmes and the televised broadcasts of the House of Commons and the House of Lords
- *Hansard*
- House of Commons *Weekly Information Bulletin*
- *Erskine May's Parliamentary Practice*

Government publications

Every year, the British government publishes thousands of books, reports and documents through Her Majesty's Stationary Office (HMSO). Its publications cover every conceivable subject involving the government, and are listed in a monthly catalogue containing a cumulative index, which is available free from HMSO Bookshops and is stocked by most libraries. It is well worth checking through as it lists reports on some of the more obscure government committees and agencies, such as the Advisory Committee on Conscientious Objectors.

Government and Industry: a business guide to Westminster, Whitehall and Brussels

This is a huge manual edited by the Rt. Hon. William Rogers and published by Kluwer which provides a wide range of information on parliamentary and governmental institutions. It covers the legislative process, including: select committees; public accounts committees; the ombudsman; parliamentary privilege and Members' interests; parliamentary information for the public; ministerial responsibilities; all-party subject groups; backbench committees. The section on Whitehall includes such things as: Ministers; parliamentary questions and speeches; direct contact with civil servants; mandarins; the House of Commons Information Service; government departments and other government sponsored bodies; nationalized industries; lobbyists and influencing policy. The European section provides information on: the Commission of the European Communities and Chefs de Cabinet; Members of the European Commission; Directorates-General and Directors-General; the Council of Ministers; the European Parliament; British MEPs. Local government in the UK is also covered. Although this book is intended for industrialists, it provides a very useful guide for anyone with an interest in government affairs.

Although MPs can ask questions in Parliament, they have no right to answers. The standard guide to Parliamentary procedure, *Erskine May*, says, 'An answer to a question cannot be insisted upon, if the answer be refuted by a minister. Any question which will cost more than £250 to answer can be refused on the grounds of "disproportionate cost". Mrs Thatcher has refused to say how many questions she has declined to answer since 1979, saying that answering that question would itself involve 'disproportionate cost'. But ministers are free to spend any amount they wish on an answer. In June 1989, the Prime Minister was asked to list the government's achievements since 1979. The reply covered 34 columns of *Hansard*, and the cost was later disclosed to have been £4600.

The Civil Service

66   The foxhole [the government] currently occupy is defensive in intent but offers no genuine protection. It offers the worst of all worlds. Whitehall's battery of confidentiality codes, conventions and statutes accumulated since 1250 amount to a leaker's charter. If Mrs Thatcher fails to consider moving her dangerous foxhole, everyone will be the loser – the public, parliament, servants, and the Cabinet. Government is a public business, not a private firm. It should conduct itself accordingly.

Leading article in *The Times*

66   The British Civil Service is a virtual monument to the obsession for secrecy that permeates the corridors of Whitehall. For example, every three months, the Civil Service prepares and circulates a list of ministerial responsibilities, showing exactly

how subjects are divided up between the different ministers in each department. Although the list is made available to MPs, it is denied to the public. In 1977, Hugo Young of the *Sunday Times* was offered a copy of the list – on condition that he didn't publish it . . .

Article in *Secrets* – newspaper of the Campaign for the
Freedom of Information

The only official guide to the Civil Service is the *Civil Service Yearbook*, which provides a surprisingly detailed profile of each government department including the names, office addresses and telephone numbers of key civil servants. It also gives detailed information on the Royal households; parliamentary offices; libraries; museums and galleries; research councils and 'other organizations'. It concludes with an index of individual civil servants and salary tables.

However, the definitive authority on the subject of Whitehall is undoubtedly Peter Hennessy's book *Whitehall*, published by Secker and Warburg. One chapter in this 800-page tome is devoted to secrecy, which Hennessy describes as 'the bonding material which holds the rambling structure of central government together'.

Political parties, lobbyists and 'think tanks'

These organizations tend to attract publicity on a regular basis; and few people will need to engage in any primary research as their activities are well documented. The Labour Research Department (*see* p. 23) regularly publishes detailed studies of right-wing pressure groups and 'think tanks' such as Aims of Industry and the Economic League. Extreme right-wing political parties and groups are monitored by the magazine *Searchlight*, 37b New Cavendish St, London W1M 8JR, which occasionally publishes supplements on its research. There are no comparable sources of information on left-wing groups and political parties, but they tend to be well covered by the mainstream press.

Trade unions

The Trade Union Handbook, published by Gower, covers most UK trade unions, trade union organizations, industrial relations bodies and other sources of information on the union movement. Trade unions are required to be registered with the Certification Office for Trade Unions & Employers

Association, 27 Wilton St, London SW1, tel. (071) 210 3733; the register there is available for public inspection. The Department of Employment publishes the *Directory of Employment Associations, Trade Unions and Joint Organizations* registered with the Department. Some trade unions are also limited companies, such as the National Union of Miners. Others operate companies for specific purposes – for example, the National Union of Railwaymen operates Unity House (Holdings) Ltd to manage its property holdings, and NUR Employees (1946) Superannuation Fund Trustees Ltd to administer its members' pension fund.

TRADE UNION CHECKLIST

Information on trade unions can be found in:

- *Trade Union Handbook*
- *Directory of Employment Associations, Trade Unions and Joint Organizations* (DoE)
- press coverage
- Companies House records

9 INTERNATIONAL RESEARCH

International research is the most lengthy, expensive and time-consuming research to be undertaken. It will be in rare circumstances that the individual citizen will need to investigate organizations or individuals outside the United Kingdom. However, there is one case where a quick and easy piece of international research was carried out by a Member of Parliament. He had tabled a parliamentary question asking for details about some aspect of Britain's contribution to NATO. The Minister of State for Defence refused to answer the question for 'security reasons'. However, the MP obtained the information a few hours later when a friend, a US Senator, faxed the details through to him. That information had been freely available in the Senate Library.

Indeed, the US Freedom of Information Act allowed American author Chuck Hanson to write a book, *US Nuclear Weapons: the secret history* (available from Aerofax, PO Box 200006, Arlington, Texas, and from Midland Counties Publications, Earl Shilton, Leicester, tel. (0455) 847091). It contains details of nuclear weapons including mathematical formulae of thermonuclear explosions and designs and drawings of existing nuclear weapons. Because of Britain's obsession with secrecy, few of us will have the opportunity of conducting that type of revealing research. The following might, though, point the researcher in the right direction:

Press coverage

International research should be started with the idea that somebody has already done that particular piece of research before, and that it has been published in a newspaper or magazine somewhere. Then the indexes of newspapers, magazines and journals listed in Chapter 7 should be consulted.

Research for Writers

This excellent handbook by Ann Hoffman (published by A. C. Black, £6.95) has an entire chapter dedicated to 'information from foreign sources' which lists principal libraries all over the world – many of which have London offices. It also provides bibliographical references for further information.

Business directories

With the approach of 1992, more and more business information will be available on European companies outside the UK, but the availability of such information is currently very unreliable. The most detailed selection can be found in central London reference libraries, including the British Library's Business Information Service, the City Business Library, Westminster Central Reference Library and Holborn Library.

European Community

The primary source of information and advice on the European Community is our elected representatives – the Members of the European Parliament (MEPs). Details of MEPs are available from local libraries or from the European Parliament's London office at 2 Queen Anne's Gate, London SW1H 9AA, tel. (071) 222 0411.

The European Community also publishes an enormous amount of information about itself. A number of 'European Documentation' booklets (40-120 pages each) are issued each year – e.g. *The ABC of Community Law, Wine in the European Community, The Common Agricultural Policy and Its Reform* – and are available from the European Community Press and Information Office, 8 Storey's Gate, London SW1P 3AT. Other EC publications (and a catalogue) can be obtained from HMSO Books (PC16), HMSO Publications Centre, 51 Nine Elms Lane, London SW8 5DR, tel. (071) 873 9090.

United Nations

The UN publishes a wide range of reports on international issues. The United Nations Association promotes the work of the UN, and its UK office is at

3 Whitehall Court, London SW1A 2EL, tel. (071) 930 2931/0679. Its London Council operates a bookshop at 23 New Quebec St, London W1H 8DH, tel. (071) 402 9029.

Interights

This campaigning organization is an international European law centre dedicated to promoting and securing the protection of human rights through the active enforcement of international rights law. It publishes reports on substantive areas of international human rights law and practice, as well as a quarterly bulletin, *Interights*, about its activities and current abuses of international human rights law. Details from Interights, Kingsway Chambers, 46 Kingsway, London WC2B 6EN, tel. (071) 242 5581.

Article 19

The international centre on censorship, Article 19 is named after Article 19 of the Universal Declaration of Human Rights, which reads: 'Everyone has the right to freedom of opinion and expression; this right includes freedom to hold opinions without interference and to seek, receive and impart information and ideas through any media regardless of frontiers.' It is an active campaigning organization that publishes books, reports and a regular bulletin. Details from Article 19, 90 Borough High St, London SE1 1LL, tel. (071) 403 4822.

Amnesty International

An international human rights organization, independent of all political, economic or religious creeds, campaigning for the abolition of capital punishment and to release prisoners of conscience. The British section of Amnesty International can be contacted at 5 Roberts Place, off Bowling Green Lane, London EC1R 0EJ, tel. (071) 251 8371.

10 RESEARCH RESOURCES

There are certain categories of information that do not fit easily in any of the other chapters in this handbook, and so they find themselves together in this miscellany.

The women's movement

The Woman's Place, Hungerford House, Victoria Embankment, London WC2, tel. (071) 836 6081, is an information, advice, support and referral organization for women. Helps individual women make contact with the women's movement, and provides a range of facilities for women including a library.

In addition to The Women's Place, there are also the following organizations:

- Lesbian Line, BM Box 1514, London WC1N 3XX, tel. (071) 837 8602

- London Women's Aid, 52–54 Featherstone St, London EC1, tel. (071) 251 6537

- National Women's Aid Federation (refuges for battered women), 374 Gray's Inn Rd, London WCl, tel. (071) 837 9316

- Onlywomen Press, 38 Mount Pleasant, London WCl, tel. (071) 837 0596

- Sheba Feminist Publishers, 488 Kingsland Rd, London E8, tel. (071) 254 1590

- Silver Moon Women's Bookshop, 68 Charing Cross Rd, London WC2, tel. (071) 836 7906

- Sisterwrite Women's Bookshop, 190 Upper St, London N1, tel. (071) 226 9782
- Women's Therapy Centre, 6 Manor Gardens, London N7, tel. (071) 263 6200

The lesbian and gay communities

The Lesbian and Gay Switchboard ((071) 837 7324) operates the UK's central lesbian and gay information and advice service, 24 hours a day, 365/6 days per annum. It is a confidential phone service providing information on: gay groups and the commercial scene throughout the UK; medical and legal referrals. It prepares a daily diary of events and carries an extensive file of lesbian and gay commercial services from plumbers to palmists. Lesbians can also use Lesbian Line on (071) 837 8602.

> Her Majesty's Customs and Excise has a secret list of 26 bookshops and publishers. Officers are instructed to seize and examine packages sent from abroad to any of the names on the list, which includes that of the lesbian and gay bookshop Gay's the Word. A Customs spokesman said: 'The document is not secret. It is restricted. I'm not confirming that it is an official secret. I cannot discuss it.'

Beneath the City Streets

This book by Peter Laurie (published by Granada) traces the ten-mile network of secret government shelters and tunnels below the streets of London. Buildings thought to have access to this network include the Telecom Tower, Centre Point, New Scotland Yard, London Transport Head-quarters and the Admiralty; there is a particularly heavy concentration around Victoria St, London SW1. The perfect read for any real-life conspiracy theorist. This same topic is also covered in Duncan Campbell's *Warplan UK* (Burnett Books).

UFOs

The British UFO Research Association (BUFORA) investigates UFO phenomena, holds public meetings and publishes the *Flying Saucer Review*. Further information on this group can be found in the directories *Centres and Bureaux* and *Directory of British Associations*.

Fanclubs

Fanclubs 88: the who's who of pop stars ('hours of entertainment with the real stars of pop') lists star profiles, the addresses of hundreds of fanclubs, hot tips and cool facts.

Gnomes

The Gnome Reserve, West Putford, North Devon, is home to over 1000 gnomes living happily in an area of birchwood by a stream, which is open to the public (admission free). The reserve publishes a newsletter for gnome lovers of all ages – *Gnome News*.

Appendix 1
ORGANIZATIONS

Amnesty International (British Section)
5 Roberts Place
off Bowling Green Lane
London EC1R 0EJ
Tel. (071) 251 8371

Article 19
90 Borough High St
London SE1 1LL
Tel. (071) 403 4822

Association of Community Health Councils
30 Drayton Park
London N5 1PB
Tel. (071) 609 8405

British Dental Association
64 Wimpole St
London W1M 8AL
Tel. (071) 935 0875

British Library Newspaper Library
Colindale Ave
London NW9 5HE
Tel. (071) 636 1544 ext. 73353 (general inquiries)
    (071) 323 7353 (general inquiries)

(071) 636 1544 ext. 7355 (photocopy inquiries)
(071) 636 1544 ext. 7676 *or* (071) 323 7676 (inquiries on specific items)

British Medical Association
BMA House
Tavistock Square
London WC1H 9JR
Tel. (071) 387 4499

Campaign Against the Arms Trade
11 Goodwin St
London N4 3HQ
Tel. (071) 281 0297

Campaign for Freedom of Information
3 Endsleigh St
London WC1H 0DD
Tel. (071) 278 9686

Campaign for Press and Broadcasting Freedom
9 Poland St
London W1V 3DG
Tel. (071) 437 2795

CCN Systems
Talbot House
Talbot St
Nottingham NG1 5HF
Tel. (0602) 410888

Centre for Alternative Industrial and Technological Systems (CAITS)
404 Camden Rd
London N7 0SJ
Tel. (071) 607 7079/700 0362

Charity Commission
St Alban's House
57-60 Haymarket
London SW1Y 4QX

Tel. (071) 210 3000
or
Graeme House
Derby Square
Liverpool L2 7SB
Tel. (051) 227 3191

College of Health
18 Victoria Park Square
London E2 9PF
Tel. (081) 980 6263

Community Rights Project
5-11 Lavington St
London SE1 0NZ
Tel. (071) 928 5538

Companies House
55 City Road
London EC1Y 1BB
Tel. (071) 253 9393
or
Crown Way
Cardiff CF4 3UZ
Tel. (0222) 388588
or
100-102 George St
Edinburgh EH2 3DJ
Tel. (031) 225 5774
or
Companies Registration Office
IDB House
Chichester St
Belfast BT1 4JX
Tel. (0232) 234488

Companies Investigation Branch
Department of Trade & Industry
Room 323
Ashdown House

123 Victoria St
London SW1E 6RB
Tel. (071) 215 5000

Council for the Protection of Rural England
4 Hobart Place
London SW1W 0HY
Tel. (071) 235 9481

The Countryside Commission
19/23 Albert Rd
Manchester M19 2EQ
Tel. (061) 224 6287

Data Protection Registrar
Springfield House
Water Lane
Wilmslow
Cheshire SK9 5AX
Tel. (0625) 535777

Driver and Vehicle Licensing Centre
Swansea SA99 1AA
Tel. (0792) 782576

Emergency Planning Information Centre
Room 326A
The Old Town Hall
Euston Rd
London NW1 2RU
Tel. (071) 860 5747

European Parliament (London office)
2 Queen Anne's Gate
London SW1H 9AA
Tel. (071) 222 0411

Friends of the Earth
26-28 Underwood St
London N1 7JQ

Tel. (071) 490 1555

Gay Switchboard
See Lesbian and Gay Switchboard

General Optical Council
41 Harley St
London W1N 2DJ
Tel. (071) 580 3898

General Register Office
(births, deaths & marriages)
St Catherine's House
10 Kingsway
London WC2B 6JP
Tel. (071) 242 0262

Health Service Ombudsman for England
Church House
Great Smith St
London SW1P 3BW
Tel. (071) 212 7676

Health Service Ombudsman for Scotland
2nd Floor
11 Melville Crescent
Edinburgh EH3 7LU
Tel. (031) 225 7465

Health Service Ombudsman for Wales
4th Floor
Pearl Assurance House
Greyfriars Rd
Cardiff CF1 3AG
Tel. (0222) 394621

Infolink
Coombe Cross
2-4 South End
Croydon

Surrey CR0 1DL
Tel. (081) 686 7777

Institute for Complementary Medicine
21 Portland Place
London W1N 3HF
Tel. (071) 636 9543

Interights
Kingsway Chambers
46 Kingsway
London WC2B 6EN
Tel. (071) 242 5581

Labour Research Department
78 Blackfriars Rd
London SE1 8HF
Tel. (071) 928 3649

Land Registry
32 Lincoln's Inn Fields
London WC2A 3PH
Tel. (071) 405 3488

Lesbian and Gay Switchboard
BM Switchboard
London WC1N 3XX
Tel. (071) 837 7324 (24 hours)

***Lobster* Magazine**
214 Westbourne Avenue
Hull HU5 3JB

London Hazards Centre
308 Gray's Inn Rd
London WC1X 8DS
Tel. (071) 837 5605

National Council for Civil Liberties (NCCL)
21 Tabard St

London SE1 4LA
Tel. (071) 403 3888

National Council for Voluntary Organizations
26 Bedford Square
London WC1B 3HU
Tel. (071) 636 4066

National Union of Journalists
Acorn House
314 Gray's Inn Rd
London WC1X 8DP
Tel. (071) 278 7916

The Open Spaces Society
25a Bell St
Henley-on-Thames
Oxon RG9 2BA
Tel. (0491) 573535

Peace Pledge Union
Dick Sheppard House
6 Endsleigh St
London WC1H 0DX
Tel. (071) 387 5501

Planning Aid for London
100 Minories
London EC3N 1JY
Tel. (071) 702 0051

Public Records Office
Chancery Lane
London WC2
Tel. (071) 876 3444
or
Ruskin Ave
Kew
Richmond
Surrey TW9 4DU

Tel. (081) 876 3444

The Ramblers' Association
1-5 Wandsworth Rd
London SW8 2XX
Tel. (071) 582 6826

Registry of Friendly Societies
15 Great Marlborough St
London W1V 2AX
Tel. (071) 437 9992
Inquiries: (071) 494 6502

Salvation Army Social Services
Investigation Department
105-109 Judd St
King's Cross
London WC1H 9TS
Tel. (071) 387 2772

Services to Community Action and Trade Unions (SCAT)
1 Sidney St
Sheffield S1 4RG
Tel. (0742) 726683

Social Audit
PO Box 111
London NW1 8XG
(071) 586 7771

Somerset House
Strand
London WC2R 1LP
Tel. (071) 405 7641

SpyBASE
Micro Associates
PO Box 5369
Arlington
VA 22205

USA

Town and Country Planning Association
17 Carlton House Terrace
London SW1Y 5AS
Tel. (071) 930 8903

Transport 2000
Walkden House
10 Melton St
London NW1 2EJ
Tel. (071) 388 8386

United Nations Association
3 Whitehall Court
London SW1A 2EL
Tel. (071) 930 2931/0679

University of Bradford School of Peace Studies
University of Bradford
Bradford 7
West Yorkshire BD7 1DP
Tel. (0274) 733466

The Woman's Place
Hungerford House
Victoria Embankment
London WC2
Tel. (071) 836 6081

APPENDIX 2
LIBRARIES AND ARCHIVES

There are thousands of public libraries throughout the UK, and the range of information they stock will vary considerably. Listed below are 50 of the key reference libraries around the UK and an outline of the comprehensive service provided by the British Library Business Information Service. There are, however, thousands more libraries kept by public bodies, private companies and organizations that may be able to provide assistance with specialized research. Many of them are listed in the *Aslib Directory of Information Sources in the United Kingdom*, which comes in two parts: Volume 1 covers science, technology and commerce (from 'Accident Research Unit' to 'Zoological Society of London'); Volume 2 covers social sciences, medicine and the humanities (from 'Aberdeen Angus Cattle Society' to 'Zip Fastener Manufacturers Association'). Another directory in this field is *British Archives: a guide to archive resources in the United Kingdom*. It lists over 700 public libraries and archives, and tends to cover specialist and less well-known institutions, alongside the larger libraries and country record office network.

British Library
Business Information Service
25 Southampton Buildings
London WC2A 1AW
Tel. (071) 323 7454 (brief inquiry service 9.30–5.00, Monday–Friday)
(071) 323 7979 (online data base search service 10.00–5.00,
Monday–Friday)
(071) 323 7979 (charged research service 10.00–5.00, Monday–Friday)
(071) 636 1544 (main switchboard)

Telex: 266959 SCIREF G
Fax: (071) 323 7495
BT Gold: (81) BL1404
Opening hours: 9.30 am to 9.00 pm, Monday to Friday
10.00 am to 1.00 pm, Saturday

The Business Information Service of the British Library is based at the Science Reference and Information Service (SIRIS) in Holborn, central London, and was set up in 1981 in response to demands for a national business information service.

The Service acts as a back-up to local information resources or as a principal resource. Using the extensive holdings of UK and overseas publications in the British Library, staff can extract reference information quickly, advise on the use of business literature and suggest other organizations to contact. The collections are freely available for reference without formality, but extensive research may require a personal visit to the library. Staff can advise whether a visit would be worthwhile.

Business information may be obtained from a variety of sources held there, including directories, newspapers, company card services, market research reports, journals, trade catalogues and online data bases. Personal callers to the library receive help with their inquiries from specialist staff between 9.30 am and 5.00 pm, Monday to Friday, and a telephone line for very brief inquiries is available during those hours.

A more extensive business information service and an online data base searching service are also offered, but at a cost; further details are available on (071) 323 7979. In addition, there is a photocopy service and a loan service of some stock through membership of the British Library Document Supply Centre. Contact with the Business Information Service can be made by post, telephone, telex, fax or British Telecom Gold. Publications based on the stock held in the library are issued regularly, and courses on the use of business research materials stock are held three or four times a year.

Public libraries

Some business and technical information should be available from any public reference library, and the only way to find out what is available in any locality is to visit the local library and have a look. Most librarians are very pleased to give a guided tour of their stock, and should be quizzed about their 'hidden' stock, such as files on local organizations, press cuttings files, local history collection, and the like. The following lists 47 of the main reference libraries throughout the UK which will stock a range of business and technical publications. Those marked with an * are listed by the British Library Science Reference and Information Service (SIRIS) as key sources of business information in the UK:

Aberdeen*
Commercial Library
Aberdeen Central Libraries
Rosemount Viaduct
Aberdeen AB9 1GU
Tel. (0224) 634622

Belfast*
Commercial Department
Belfast Public Libraries
Royal Ave
Belfast BT1 1EA
Tel. (0232) 243233

Birmingham*
Central Library
Chamberlain Square
Birmingham B3 3HQ
Tel. (021) 235 4511

Bradford
Central Library
Bradford City Libraries
Prince's Way
Bradford BD1 1NN
Tel. (0274) 753656

Bristol
Central Library
Avon County Libraries
College Green
Bristol BS1 5TL
Tel. (0272) 276121

Cambridge
Central Library
7 Lion Yard
Cambridge CB2 3QD
Tel. (0223) 65252

Carlisle
Reference Department
Central Library
Cumbria County Library
11 Globe Lane
Carlisle CO3 8NX
Tel. (0228) 24166

Chatham
Reference Library
Riverside
Chatham ME4 5SN
Tel. (0634) 43589

Chelmsford
Information Librarian
Essex County Library
Goldlay Gardens
Chelmsford CM2 0EW
Tel. (0245) 84981

Coventry
Reference Section
Coventry Central Library
Bayley Lane
Coventry CV1 5RG
Tel. (0203) 25555

Derby
Central Library
Derbyshire County Library
The Warwick
Derby DE1 1HS
Tel. (0332) 31111

Edinburgh
Reference Section
Edinburgh Central Library
George IV Bridge
Edinburgh EH1 1EG
Tel. (031) 225 5584

Exeter
Central Library
Castle St
Exeter EX4 3PQ
Tel. (0392) 77977

Glasgow*
Glasgow City Library
Mitchell Library
North St
Glasgow G3 7DN
Tel. (041) 221 7030

Gloucester
Reference Library
Gloucestershire County Council
Brunswick Rd
Gloucester GL1 1HT
Tel. (0452) 426977

Hatfield (Herts.)
Commercial Information Service
Hatfield Polytechnic
PO Box 110
Hatfield AL10 9HD
Tel. (07072) 79679

Hull
Central Library
Humberside County Library
Albion St
Hull HU1 3TF
Tel. (0842) 224040

Ipswich
Central Library
Northgate St
Ipswich IP1 3DE
Tel. (0473) 214370

Leeds
Leeds City Libraries
32 York St
Leeds LS9 8TD
Tel. (0532) 462017

Leicester
Central Library
Leicestershire County Council
Bishop St
Leicester LE1 6AA
Tel. (0533) 556699

Liverpool*
Central Library
Liverpool City Libraries
William Brown St
Liverpool L3 8EW
Tel. (051) 207 2147

London
City Business Library*
Furness House
106 Fenchurch St
London EC3M 5JB
Tel. (071) 638 8215/6

Ealing Reference Library
Central Library
103 Ealing Broadway Centre
London W5 5JY
Tel. (081) 567 3656

Holborn Reference Library*
32-38 Theobald's Rd
London WC1X 8PA
Tel. (071) 405 2705/6

Lambeth Reference Library
Tate Library
Brixton
London SW2 1JQ
Tel. (071) 274 7451

Lewisham Reference Library
140 Lewisham Way
London SE14 6PF
Tel. (081) 692 1162

Southwark Reference Library
155-157 Walworth Rd
London SE17 1RS
Tel. (071) 703 3324/5529/6514

Westminster Central Reference Library*
St Martin's St
London WC2H 7HP
Tel. (071) 798 2034/2036

Luton
Central Library
Bedfordshire County Library
Bridge St
Luton LU1 2NG
Tel. (0582) 30161

Manchester*
Central Library
Manchester City Libraries
St Peter's Square
Manchester M2 5PD
Tel. (061) 236 9422

Middlesbrough
Central Library
Cleveland County Library
Victoria Square
Middlesbrough TS1 2AY
Tel. (0642) 248155

Newcastle-upon-Tyne
Central Library
Newcastle City Libraries
Princess Square
Newcastle-upon-Tyne NE99 1DX
Tel. (091) 261 0691

Northampton
Reference Library
Northampton Libraries
Abington St
Northampton NN1 2BA
Tel. (0604) 33628/30403

Nottingham*
Business Library
Nottinghamshire County Library
Angel Row
Nottingham NG1 6HP
Tel. (0602) 412121

Oxford
Reference Library
Oxfordshire County Libraries
Westgate
Oxford OX1 1DJ
Tel. (0865) 815509

Plymouth
Central Library
Devon Library Services
Drakes Circus
Plymouth PL4 8AL

Tel. (0752) 264675

Pontypridd
Library
Polytechnic of Wales
Pontypridd
Mid Glamorgan CF37 1DL
Tel. (0443) 405133

Portsmouth*
Reference Department
Central Library
Guildhall Square
Portsmouth PO1 2DX
Tel. (0705) 819311/7

Reading
Reference Department
Berkshire County Library
Abbey Square
Reading RG1 3BQ
Tel. (0734) 509245

Rugby
Business Information Unit
Warwickshire County Library
Rugby Library
St Matthew's St
Rugby CV21 3BZ
Tel. (0788) 811355

Sheffield*
Business Library
Sheffield City Libraries
Surrey St
Sheffield S1 1XZ
Tel. (0742) 734736/8

Shrewsbury
Central Information and Reference Unit

Shropshire County Library
1a Castle St
Shrewsbury SY1 2AQ
Tel. (0743) 241207/8

Slough
Reference Library
Berkshire County Library
High St
Slough SL1 1EA
Tel. (0753) 35166

Southampton
Reference Library
Hampshire County Library
Civic Centre
Southampton SO9 4XP
Tel. (0703) 832462/3

Swansea
Central Reference Library
Swansea City Libraries
Alexandra Rd
Swansea SA1 4PJ
Tel. (0792) 55521

Truro
Reference and Information Service
Cornwall County Library
Union Place
Truro TR1 1EP
Tel. (0872) 72702

Winchester
Reference Library
81 North Walls
Winchester SO23 8BY
Tel. (0962) 60644

APPENDIX 3
COMPLAINTS: WHERE TO GO FOR HELP

There are a wide range of specialist organizations that represent various groups of people: the professions, traders, consumers, ethnic groups – and so on. They are specialists in their own particular fields, and can help with complaints and queries about more detailed information.

Advertising Standards Authority
Brook House
Torrington Place
London WC1E 7HN
Tel.(071) 580 5555

Advisory Committee on Telecommunications (Oftel)
Atlantic House
Holborn Viaduct
London EC1N 2HQ
Tel. (071) 353 4020

Advisory, Conciliation and Arbitration Service (ACAS)
27 Wilton St
London SW1
Tel. (071) 388 5100

Air Transport Users Committee
129 Kingsway
London WC2B 6NN
Tel. (071) 242 3882

Architects Registration Council of the United Kingdom (ARCUK)
73 Hallam St
London W1N 6EE
Tel. (071) 580 5861

Association of British Insurers
Aldermary House
Queen St
London EC4N 1TT
Tel. (071) 248 4477

Association of Optical Practitioners
233-234 Blackfriars Rd
London SE1 8NW
Tel. (071) 261 9661

Banking Ombudsman
Citadel House
Fetter Lane
London EC4A 1BR
Tel. (071) 583 1395

Bar Council
11 South Square
Gray's Inn
London WC1R 5EL
Tel. (071) 242 0082

British Airports Authority plc
Corporate Office
130 Wilton St
London SW1
Tel. (071) 834 9449

British Board of Film Classification
3 Soho Square
London W1V 5DE
Tel. (071) 439 7961

British Broadcasting Corporation (BBC)
Broadcasting House
Portland Place
London W1A 4WW
Tel. (071) 580 4468

British Insurance Brokers Association (BIBA)
BIBA House
14 Bevis Marks
London EC3A 7NT
Tel. (071) 623 9043

Broadcasting Complaints Commission
Grosvenor Gardens House
35 Grosvenor Gardens
London SW1W 0BS
Tel. (071) 630 1966

Building Societies Association
3 Savile Row
London W1X 1AF
Tel. (071) 437 0655

Central Office of the Industrial Tribunals
England and Wales
93 Ebury Bridge Rd
London SW1W 8QQ
Tel. (071) 730 9161

Scotland
St Andrews House
141 West Nile St
Glasgow G1 2RU
Tel. (041) 331 1601

Northern Ireland
Bedford House
16-22 Bedford St
Belfast BT2 7NR
Tel. (0232) 227666

Central Transport Consultative Committee
Golden Cross House
Duncannon St
London WC2N 4JF
Tel. (071) 839 7338

Chartered Association of Certified Accountants
29 Lincoln's Inn Fields
London WC2A 3EE
Tel. (071) 242 6855

Chartered Institute of Arbitrators
75 Cannon Street
London EC4N 5BH
Tel. (071) 236 8761

Chartered Institute of Public Finance and Accountancy
3 Robert St
London WC2N 6BH
Tel. (071) 895 8823

Children's Legal Centre
20 Compton Terrace
London N1 2UN
Tel. (071) 359 6251

Commission for Local Administration
England
21 Queen Anne's Gate
London SW1H 9BU
Tel. (071) 222 5622

Wales
Derwent House
Court Rd
Bridgend
Mid Glamorgan CF31 1BN
Tel. (0656) 61325

Scotland
5 Shandwick Place
Edinburgh EH2 4RG
Tel. (031) 229 4472

Commission for Racial Equality
Eliot House
10-12 Arlington St
London SW1E 5EH
Tel. (071) 828 7022

Commissioner for Complaints
33 Wellington Place
Belfast BT1 6HN
Tel. (0232) 33821

Consumers' Association
2 Marylebone Rd
London NW1 4DX
Tel. (071) 486 5544

Council for Professions Supplementary to Medicine
Park House
184 Kennington Park Rd
London SE11 4BU
Tel. (071) 582 0866

Department of Education and Science
Elizabeth House
39 York Rd
London SE1 7PH
Tel. (071) 928 9222

Department of the Environment
2 Marsham St
London SW1P 3EB
Tel. (071) 212 3434

Department of the Environment for Northern Ireland
Parliament Building

Stormont
Belfast BT4 3SY
Tel. (0232) 63210

Department of Trade and Industry
1-19 Victoria St
London SW1H 0ET
Tel. (071) 215 7877

Employment Appeals Tribunal
4 St James's Square
London SW1Y 4JU
Tel. (071) 210 3000

Equal Opportunities Commission
England
Overseas House
Quay St
Manchester M3 3HN
Tel. (061) 833 9244

Northern Ireland
Lindsay House
Callendar St
Belfast BT1 5DT
Tel. (0282) 240020

Scotland
249 West George St
Glasgow G2 4QE
Tel. (041) 226 4591

Wales
Caerwys House
Windsor Place
Cardiff CF1 1LB
Tel. (0222) 43552

European Commission on Human Rights
Council of Europe
67006 Strasbourg Cedex

France
Tel. (010 33) 88 614 961

General Council and Register of Osteopaths
1 Suffolk St
London SW1Y 4HG
tel. (071) 839 2060

General Dental Council
37 Wimpole St
London W1M 8DQ
Tel. (071) 486 2171

General Medical Council
44 Hallam St
London W1N 6AE
Tel. (071) 580 7642

General Optical Council
41 Harley St
London W1N 6AE
Tel. (071) 580 3898

Health Service Commissioner
England
Church House
Great Smith St
London SW1P 3BW
Tel. 276 3000

Scotland
11 Melville Crescent
Edinburgh EH3 7LU
Tel. (031) 225 7465

Wales
Pearl Assurance House
Greyfriars Rd
Cardiff CF1 3AG
Tel. (0222) 394621

Home Office
50 Queen Anne's Gate
London SW1H 9AT
Tel. (071) 213 3000

Housing Corporation
Maple House
149 Tottenham Court Rd
London W1P 0BN
Tel. (071) 387 9466

Incorporated Society of Valuers and Auctioneers
3 Cadogan Gate
London SW1X 0AS
Tel. (071) 235 2282

Independent Broadcasting Authority
70 Brompton Rd
London SW3 1EY
Tel. (071) 584 7011

HM Inspectorate of Pollution
3 East Grinstead House
London Rd
East Grinstead
West Sussex
Tel. (0342) 312016

Institute of Chartered Accountants
England and Wales
Moorgate Place
London EC2P 2BJ
Tel. (071) 628 7060

Northern Ireland
11 Donegal Square South
Belfast BT1 5JE
Tel. (0232) 221600

Scotland
27 Queen St

Edinburgh EH2 1LA
Tel. (031) 225 5673

Institute of Cost and Executive Accountants
63 Portland Place
London W1N 4AB
Tel. (071) 637 4716

Insurance Brokers Registration Council
15 St Helen's Place
London EC3A 6DS
Tel. (071) 588 4387

Insurance Ombudsman Bureau
31 Southampton Row
London WC1B 5HJ
Tel. (071) 242 8613

Law Society
England and Wales
8 Bream's Buildings
London EC4A 1HP
Tel. (071) 242 1222

Northern Ireland
Royal Courts of Justice
Chichester St
Belfast BT1 3JZ
Tel. (0232) 231614

Scotland
26-27 Drumsheugh Gardens
Edinburgh EH3 7YR
Tel. (031) 226 7411

Lay Observer
England and Wales
Royal Courts of Justice
Strand
London WC2A 2LL
Tel. (071) 405 7641

Northern Ireland
IDB House
64 Chichester St
Belfast BT1 4LE
Tel. (0232) 233233

Scotland
22 Melville St
Edinburgh EH3 7NS
Tel. (031) 225 3236

Lloyds of London
1986 Building
Lime St
London EC3
Tel. (071) 623 7100

London Regional Passengers Committee
Golden Cross House
2 Duncannon St
London WC2N 4JF
Tel. (071) 839 1898

Mail Users' Association
6 Whitgift St
Croydon CR0 1DH
Tel. (081) 681 7196

Mental Health Act Commission
Hepburn House
Marsham St
London SW1 4HW
Tel. (071) 211 8061

Mental Welfare Commission for Scotland
22 Melville St
Edinburgh EH3 7NS
Tel. (031) 225 7034

National Association of Estate Agents
Arbon House
21 Jury St
Warwick CV34 4EH
Tel. (0926) 496800

National Board for Nursing, Midwifery and Health Visiting
England
Victory House
170 Tottenham Court Rd
London W1P 0HA
Tel. (071) 388 3131

Northern Ireland
126 Belmont Rd
Belfast BT4 2AT
Tel. (0232) 652713

Scotland
22 Queen St
Edinburgh EH2 1JX
Tel. (031) 226 7371

Wales
Pearl Assurance House
Greyfriars Rd
Cardiff CF1 3AG
Tel. (0222) 395535

Office of Fair Trading
Field House
Breams Buildings
London EC4A 1PR
Tel. (071) 242 2858

Oftel
see Advisory Committee on Telecommunications

Parliamentary Commissioner for Administration
England, Wales, Scotland
Church House

Great Smith St
London SW1P 3BW
Tel. (071) 276 3000

Northern Ireland
33 Wellington Place
Belfast BT1 6HN
Tel. (0232) 33821

Police Complaints Authority
10 Great George St
London SW1P 3AB
Tel. (071) 273 6450

Post Office National Council
England
Waterloo Bridge House
Waterloo Rd
London SE1 8UA
Tel. (071) 928 9458

Northern Ireland
22 Great Victoria St
Belfast BT2 7PU
Tel. (0232) 244113

Scotland
Alhambra House
45 Waterloo St
Glasgow G2 6AT
Tel. (041) 248 2855

Wales
2 Park Grove
Cardiff CF1 3BN
Tel. (0222) 374028

Press Council
1 Salisbury Square
London EC4Y 8AE
Tel. (071) 353 1248

Royal Institute of British Architects
66 Portland Place
London W1N 4AD
Tel. (071) 580 5533

Royal Institute of Chartered Surveyors
12 Great George St
London SW1P 3AD
Tel. (071) 222 7000

Stock Exchange
The Stock Exchange
London EC2
Tel. (071) 588 2355

Welsh Office
Crown Buildings
Cathays Park
Cardiff CF1 3NQ
Tel. (0222) 825111

APPENDIX 4
DATA PROTECTION ACT, 1984 (EXTRACT)

PART III

RIGHTS OF DATA SUBJECTS

21.   Right of access to personal data

(1)   Subject to the provisions of this section, an individual shall be entitled—

- (a) to be informed by any data user whether the data held by him include personal data of which that individual is the data subject; and
- (b) to be supplied by any data user with a copy of the information constituting any such personal data held by him;

and where any of the information referred to in paragraph (b) above is expressed in terms which are not intelligible without explanation the information shall be accompanied by an explanation of those terms.

(2)   A data user shall not be obliged to supply any information under subsection (1) above except in response to a request in writing and on payment of such fee (not exceeding the prescribed maximum) as he may require; but a request for information under both paragraphs of that subsection shall be treated as a single request and a request for information under paragraph (a) shall, in the absence of any indication to the contrary, be treated as extending also to information under paragraph (b).

(3)   In the case of a data user having separate entries in the register in respect of data held for different purposes a separate request must be made and a separate fee paid under this section in respect of the data to which each entry relates.

(4)   A data user shall not be obliged to comply with a request under this section—
   (a) unless he is supplied with such information as he may reasonably require in order to satisfy himself as to the identity of the person making the request and to locate the information which he seeks; and
   (b) if he cannot comply with the request without disclosing information relating to another individual who can be identified from that information, unless he is satisfied that the other individual has consented to the disclosure of the information to the person making the request.

(5)   In paragraph (b) of subsection (4) above the reference to information relating to another individual includes a reference to information identifying that individual as the source of the information sought by the request; and that paragraph shall not be construed as excusing a data user from supplying so much of the information sought by the request as can be supplied without disclosing the identity of the other individual concerned, whether by the omission of names or other identifying particulars or otherwise.

(6)   A data user shall comply with a request under this section within forty days of receiving the request or, if later, receiving the information referred to in paragraph (a) of subsection (4) above and, in a case where it is required, the consent referred to in paragraph (b) of that subsection.

(7)   The information to be supplied pursuant to a request under this section shall be supplied by reference to the data in question at the time when the request is received except that it may take account of any amendment or deletion made between that time and the time when the information is supplied, being an amendment or deletion that would have been made regardless of the receipt of the request.

(8)   If a court is satisfied on the application of any person who has made a request under the foregoing provisions of this section that the data user in question has failed to comply with the request in contravention of those provisions, the court may order him to comply with the request: but a court shall not make an order under this subsection if it considers that it would in

all the circumstances be unreasonable to do so, whether because of the frequency with which the applicant has made requests to the data user under those provisions or for any other reason.

(9)   The Secretary of State may by order provide for enabling a request under this section to be made on behalf of any individual who is incapable by reason of mental disorder of managing his own affairs.

22.   Compensation for inaccuracy

(1)   An individual who is the subject of personal data held by a data user and who suffers damage by reason of the inaccuracy of the data shall be entitled to compensation from the data user for that damage and for any distress which the individual has suffered by reason of the inaccuracy.

(2)   In the case of data which accurately record information received or obtained by the data user from the data subject or a third party, subsection (1) above does not apply if the following requirements have been complied with—

  (a) the data indicate that the information was received or obtained as aforesaid or the information has not been extracted from the data except in a form which includes an indication to that effect; and

  (b) if the data subject has notified the data user that he regards the information as incorrect or misleading, an indication to the effect has been included in the data or the information has not been extracted from the data except in a form which includes an indication to that effect.

(3)   In proceedings brought against any person by virtue of this section it shall be a defence to prove that he had taken such care as in all the circumstances was reasonably required to ensure the accuracy of the data at the material time.

(4)   Data are inaccurate for the purposes of this section if incorrect or misleading as to any matter of fact.

23.   Compensation for loss or unauthorized disclosure

(1)   An individual who is the subject of personal data held by a data user or in respect of which services are provided by a person carrying on a computer bureau and who suffers damage by reason of—

  (a) the loss of the data;

(b) the destruction of the data without the authority of the data user or, as the case may be, of the person carrying on the bureau; or

(c) subject to subsection (2) below, the disclosure of the data, or access having been obtained to the data, without such authority as afore-said,

shall be entitled to compensation from the data user or, as the case may be, the person carrying on the bureau for that damage and for any distress which the individual has suffered by reason of the loss, destruction, disclosure or access.

(2) In the case of a registered data user, subsection (1)(c) above does not apply to disclosure to, or access by, any person falling within a description specified pursuant to section 4(3)(d) above in an entry in the register relating to that data user.

(3) In proceedings brought against any person by virtue of this section it shall be a defence to prove that he had taken such care as in all the circumstances was reasonably required to prevent the loss, destruction, disclosure or access in question.

24.   Rectification and erasure

(1) If a court is satisfied on the application of a data subject that personal data held by a data user of which the applicant is the subject are inaccurate within the meaning of section 22 above, the court may order the rectification or erasure of the data and of any data held by the data user and containing an expression of opinion which appears to the court to be based on the inaccurate data.

(2) Subsection (1) above applies whether or not the data accurately record information received or obtained by the data user from the data subject or a third party but where the data accurately record such information, then—

(a) if the requirements mentioned in section 22(2) above have been complied with, the court may, instead of making an order under subsection (1) above, make an order requiring the data to be supplemented by such statement of the true facts relating to the matters dealt with by the data as the court may approve; and

(b) if all or any of those requirements have not been complied with, the court may, instead of making an order under that subsection, make such order as it thinks fit for securing compliance with those requirements with or without a further order requiring the data to be supplemented by such a statement as is mentioned in paragraph (a) above.

(3) If a court is satisfied on the application of a data subject—

   (a) that he has as suffered damage by reason of the disclosure of personal data, or of access having been obtained to personal data, in circumstances entitling him to compensation under section 23 above; and

   (b) that there is a substantial risk of further disclosure of or access to the data without such authority as is mentioned in that section,

the court may order the erasure of the data; but, in the case of data in respect of which services were being provided by a person carrying on a computer bureau, the court shall not make such an order unless such steps as are reasonably practicable have been taken for notifying the person for whom those services were provided and giving him an opportunity to be heard.

25.   Jurisdiction and procedure

(1) The jurisdiction conferred by sections 21 and 24 above shall be exercisable by the High Court or a county court or, in Scotland, by the Court Session or the sheriff.

(2) For the purpose of determining any question whether an applicant under subsection (8) of section 21 above is entitled to the information which he seeks (including any question whether any relevant data are exempt from that section by virtue of Part IV of this Act) a court may require the information constituting any data held by the data user to be made available for its own inspection but shall not, pending the determination of that question in the applicant's favour, require the information sought by the applicant to be disclosed to him or his representatives whether by discovery (or, in Scotland, recovery) or otherwise.

PART **IV**

EXEMPTIONS

26.   Preliminary

(1)   References in any provision of Part II or III of this Act to personal data do not include references to data which by virtue of this Part of this Act are exempt from that provision.

(2)   In this Part of this Act 'the subject access provisions' means—
  (a)   section 21 above; and
  (b)   any provision of Part II of this Act conferring a power on the Registrar to the extent to which it is exercisable by reference to paragraph (a) of the seventh data protection principle.

(3)   In this Part of this Act 'the non-disclosure provisions' means—
  (a)   sections 5(2)(d) and 15 above; and
  (b)   any provision of Part II of this Act conferring a power on the Registrar to the extent to which it is exercisable by reference to any data protection principle inconsistent with the disclosure in question.

(4)   Except as provided by this Part of this Act the subject access provisions shall apply notwithstanding any enactment or rule of law prohibiting or restricting the disclosure, or authorizing the withholding, of information.

27.   National security

(1)   Personal data are exempt from the provisions of Part II of this Act and of sections 21 to 24 above if the exemption is required for the purpose of safeguarding national security.

(2)   Any question whether the exemption mentioned in subsection (1) above is or at any time was required for the purpose there mentioned in respect of any personal data shall be determined by a Minister of the Crown: and a certificate signed by a Minister of the Crown certifying that the exemption is or at any time was so required shall be conclusive evidence of that fact.

(3)   Personal data which are not exempt under subsection (1) above are exempt from the non-disclosure provisions in any case in which the disclosure of the data is for the purpose of safeguarding national security.

(4)   For the purposes of subsection (3) above a certificate signed by a Minister of the Crown certifying that personal data are or have been disclosed for the purpose mentioned in that subsection shall be conclusive evidence of that fact.

(5)   A document purporting to be such a certificate as is mentioned in this section shall be received in evidence and deemed to be such a certificate unless the contrary is proved.

(6)   The powers conferred by this section on a Minister of the Crown shall not be exercisable except by a Minister who is a member of the Cabinet or by the Attorney General or the Lord Advocate.

28.   Crime and taxation

(1)   Personal data held for any of the following purposes—
    (a)   the prevention or detection of crime;
    (b)   the apprehension or prosecution of offenders; or
    (c)   the assessment or collection of any tax or duty,

are exempt from the subject access provisions in any case in which the application of those provisions to the data would be likely to prejudice any of the matters mentioned in this subsection.

(2)   Personal data which—
    (a)   are held for the purpose of discharging statutory functions; and
    (b)   consist of information obtained for such a purpose from a person who had it in his possession for any of the purposes mentioned in subsection (1) above,

are exempt from the subject access provisions to the same extent as personal data held for any of the purposes mentioned in that subsection.

(3)   Personal data are exempt from the non-disclosure provisions in any case in which—
    (a)   the disclosure is for any of the purposes mentioned in subsection (1) above; and
    (b)   the application of those provisions in relation to the disclosure would be likely to prejudice any of the matters mentioned in that subsection;

and in proceedings against any person for contravening a provision mentioned in section 26(3)(a) above it shall be a defence to prove that he had reasonable grounds for believing that failure to make the disclosure in question would have been likely to prejudice any of those matters.

(4)   Personal data are exempt from the provisions of Part II of this Act conferring powers on the Registrar, to the extent to which they are exercisable by reference to the first data protection principle, in any case in which the application of those provisions to the data would be likely to prejudice any of the matters mentioned in subsection (1) above.

29.   Health and social work

(1)   The Secretary of State may by order exempt from the subject access provisions, or modify those provisions in relation to, personal data consisting of information as to the physical or mental health of the data subject.

(2)   The Secretary of State may by order exempt from the subject access provisions, or modify those provisions in relation to, personal data of such other descriptions as may be specified in the order, being information—

  (a) held by government departments or local authorities or by voluntary organizations or other bodies designated by or under the order; and
  (b) appearing to him to be held for, or acquired in the course of, carrying out social work in relation to the data subject or other individuals;

but the Secretary of State shall not under this subsection confer any exemption or make any modification except so far as he considers that the application to the data of those provisions (or of those provisions without modification) would be likely to prejudice the carrying out of social work.

(3)   An order under this section may make different provision in relation to data consisting of information of different descriptions.

30.   Regulation of financial services etc.

(1)   Personal data held for the purpose of discharging statutory functions to which this section applies are exempt from the subject access provisions in any case in which the application of those provisions to the data would be likely to prejudice the proper discharge of those functions.

(2)   This section applies to any functions designated for the purposes of this section by an order made by the Secretary of State, being functions conferred by or under any enactment appearing to him to be designed for protecting members of the public against financial loss due to dishonesty, incompetence or malpractice by persons concerned in the provision of banking, insurance,

investment or other financial services or in the management of companies or to the conduct of discharged or undischarged bankrupts.

31.   Judicial appointments and legal professional privilege

(1)   Personal data held by a government department are exempt from the subject access provisions if the data consist of information which has been received from a third party and is held as information relevant to the making of judicial appointments.

(2)   Personal data are exempt from the subject access provisions if the data consist of information in respect of which a claim to legal professional privilege (or, in Scotland, to confidentiality as between client and professional legal adviser) could be maintained in legal proceedings.

32.   Payrolls and accounts

(1)   Subject to subsection (2) below, personal data held by a data user only for one or more of the following purposes—

    (a)   calculating amounts payable by way of remuneration or pensions in respect of service in any employment or office or making payments of, or of sums deducted from, such remuneration or pensions; or

    (b)   keeping accounts relating to any business or other activity carried on by the data user or keeping records of purchases, sales or other transactions for the purpose of ensuring that the requisite payments are made by or to him in respect of those transactions or for the purpose of making financial or management forecasts to assist him in the conduct of any such business or activity,

are exempt from the provisions of Part II of this Act and of sections 21 to 24 above.

(2)   It shall be a condition of the exemption of any data under this section that the data are not used for any purpose other than the purpose or purposes for which they are held and are not disclosed except as permitted by subsections (3) and (4) below; but the exemption shall not be lost by any use or disclosure in breach of that condition if the data user shows that he had taken such care to prevent it as in all the circumstances was reasonably required.

(3)   Data held only for one or more of the purposes mentioned in subsection (1)(a) above may be disclosed—

(a) to any person, other than the data user, by whom the remuneration or pensions in question are payable;

(b) for the purpose of obtaining actuarial advice;

(c) for the purpose of giving information as to the persons in any employment or office for use in medical research into the health of, or injuries suffered by, persons engaged in particular occupations or working in particular places or areas;

(d) if the data subject (or a person acting on his behalf) has requested or consented to the disclosure of the data either generally or in the circumstances in which the disclosure in question is made; or

(e) if the person making the disclosure has reasonable grounds for believing that the disclosure falls within paragraph (d) above.

(4)   Data held for any of the purposes mentioned in subsection (1) above may be disclosed—

(a) for the purpose of audit or where the disclosure is for the purpose only of giving information about the data user's financial affairs; or

(b) in any case in which disclosure would be permitted by any other provision of this Part of this Act if subsection (2) above were included among the non-disclosure provisions.

(5)   In this section 'remuneration' includes remuneration in kind and 'pensions' includes gratuities or similar benefits.

33.   Domestic or other limited purposes

(1)   Personal data held by an individual and concerned only with the management of his personal, family or household affairs or held by him only for recreational purposes are exempt from the provisions of Part II of this Act of sections 21 to 24 above.

(2)   Subject to subsections (3) and (4) below—

(a) personal data held by an unincorporated members' club and relating only to the members of the club; and

(b) personal data held by a data user only for the purpose of distributing, or recording the distribution of, articles or information to the data subjects and consisting only of their names, addresses or other particulars necessary for effecting the distribution,

are exempt from the provisions of Part II of this Act and of sections 21 to 24 above.

(3)   Neither paragraph (a) nor paragraph (b) of subsection (2) above applies to personal data relating to any data subject unless he has been asked by the club or data user whether he objects to the data relating to him being held as mentioned in that paragraph and has not objected.

(4)   It shall be a condition of the exemption of any data under paragraph (b) of subsection (2) above that the data are not used for any purpose other than that for which they are held and of the exemption of any data under either paragraph of that subsection that the data are not disclosed except as permitted by subsection (5) below; but the first exemption shall not be lost by any use, and neither exemption shall be lost by any disclosure, in breach of that condition if the data user shows that he had taken such care to prevent it as in all the circumstances was reasonably required.

(5)   Data to which subsection (4) above applies may be disclosed—
    (a) if the data subject (or a person acting on his behalf) has requested or consented to the disclosure of the data either generally or in the circumstances in which the disclosure in question is made;
    (b) if the person making the disclosure has reasonable grounds for believing that the disclosure falls within paragraph (a) above; or
    (c) in any case in which disclosure would be permitted by any other provision of this Part of this Act if subsection (4) above were included among the non-disclosure provisions.

(6)   Personal data held only for—
    (a) preparing statistics; or
    (b) carrying out of research,

are exempt from the subject access provisions; but it shall be a condition of that exemption that the data are not used or disclosed for any other purpose and that the resulting statistics or the results of the research are not made available in a form which identifies the data subjects or any of them.

34.   Other exemptions

(1)   Personal data held by any person are exempt from the provisions of Part II of this Act and of sections 21 to 24 above if the data consist of information which that person is required by or under any enactment to make available to the public, whether by publishing it, making it available for inspection or otherwise and whether gratuitously or on payment of a fee.

(2)   The Secretary of State may by order exempt from the subject access provisions personal data consisting of information the disclosure of which is

prohibited or restricted by or under any enactment if he considers that the prohibition or restriction ought to prevail over those provisions in the interests of the data subject or of any other individual.

(3)   Where all the personal data relating to a data subject held by a data user (or all such data in respect of which a data user has a separate entry in the register) consist of information in respect of which the data subject is entitled to make a request to the data user under section 158 of the Consumer Credit Act 1974 (files of credit reference agencies)—

    (a) the data are exempt from the subject access provisions; and

    (b) any request in respect of the data under section 21 above shall be treated for all purposes as if it were a request under the said section 158.

(4)   Personal data are exempt from the subject access provisions if the data are kept only for the purpose of replacing other data in the event of the latter being lost, destroyed or impaired.

(5)   Personal data are exempt from the non-disclosure provisions in any case in which the disclosure is—

    (a) required by or under any enactment, by any rule of law or by the order of a court; or

    (b) made for the purpose of obtaining legal advice or for the purposes of, or in the course of, legal proceedings in which the person making the disclosure is a party or a witness.

(6)   Personal data are exempt from the non-disclosure provisions in any case in which—

    (a) the disclosure is to the data subject or a person acting on his behalf; or

    (b) the data subject or any such person has requested or consented to the particular disclosure in question; or

    (c) the disclosure is by a data user or a person carrying on a computer bureau to his servant or agent for the purpose of enabling the servant or agent to perform his functions as such; or

    (d) the person making the disclosure has reasonable grounds for believ- ing that the disclosure falls within any of the foregoing paragraphs of this subsection.

(7)   Section 4(3)(d) above does not apply to any disclosure falling within paragraph (a), (b) or (c) of subsection (6) above; and that subsection shall

apply to the restriction on disclosure in section 33(6) above as it applies to the non-disclosure provisions.

(8)   Personal data are exempt from the non-disclosure provisions in any case in which the disclosure is urgently required for preventing injury or other damage to the health of any person or persons; and in proceedings against any person for contravening a provision mentioned in section 26(3)(a) above it shall be a defence to prove that he had reasonable grounds for believing that the disclosure in question was urgently required for that purpose.

(9)   A person need not comply with a notice, request or order under the subject access provisions if compliance would expose him to proceedings for any offence other than an offence under this Act; and information disclosed by any person in compliance with such a notice, request or order shall not be admissible against him in proceedings for an offence under this Act.

35.   Examination marks

(1)   Section 21 above shall have effect subject to the provisions of this section in the case of personal data consisting of marks or other information held by a data user—
  (a) for the purpose of determining the results of an academic, profes-
       sional or other examination or of enabling the results of any such
       examination to be determined; or
  (b) in consequence of the determination of any such results.

(2)   Where the period mentioned in subsection (6) of section 21 begins before the results of the examination are announced that period shall be extended until—
  (a) the end of five months from the beginning of that period; or
  (b) the end of forty days after the date of the announcement,

whichever is the earlier.

(3)   Where by virtue of subsection (2) above a request is complied with more than forty days after the beginning of the period mentioned in subsection (6) of section 21, the information to be supplied pursuant to the request shall be supplied both by reference to the data in question at the time when the request is received and (if different) by reference to the data as from time to time held in the period beginning when the request is received and ending when it is complied with.

(4)   For the purposes of this section the results of an examination shall be treated as announced when they are first published or (if not published) when they are first made available or communicated to the candidate in question.

(5)   In this section 'examination' includes any process for determining the knowledge, intelligence, skill or ability of a candidate by reference to his performance in any test, work or other activity.

PART V

GENERAL

36.   General duties of Registrar

(1)   It shall be the duty of the Registrar so to perform his functions under this Act as to promote the observance of the data protection principles by data users and persons carrying on computer bureaux.

(2)   The Registrar may consider any complaint that any of the data protection principles or any provision of this Act has been or is being contravened and shall do so if the complaint appears to him to raise a matter of substance and to have been made without undue delay by a person directly affected; and where the Registrar considers any such complaint he shall notify the complainant of the result of his consideration and of any action which he proposes to take.

(3)   The Registrar shall arrange for the dissemination in such form and manner as he considers appropriate of such information as it may appear to him expedient to give to the public about the operation of this Act and other matters within the scope of his functions under this Act and may give advice to any person as to any of those matters.

(4)   It shall be the duty of the Registrar, where he considers it appropriate to do so, to encourage trade associations or other bodies representing data users to prepare, and to disseminate to their members, codes of practice for guidance in complying with the data protection principles.

(5)   The Registrar shall annually lay before each House of Parliament a general report on the performance of his functions under this Act and may

from time to time lay before each House of Parliament such other reports with respect to those functions as he thinks fit.

37.   Co-operation between parties to Convention

The Registrar shall be the designated authority on the United Kingdom for the purposes of Article 13 of the European Convention; and the Secretary of State may by order make provision as to the functions to be discharged by the Registrar in that capacity.

38.   Application to government departments and police

(1)   Except as provided in subsection (2) below, a government shall be subject to the same obligations and liabilities under this Act as a private person; and for the purposes of this Act each government department shall be treated as a person separate from any other government department and a person in the public service of the Crown shall be treated as a servant of the government department to which his responsibilities or duties relate.

(2)   A government department shall not be liable to prosecution under this Act but—

    (a)   sections 5(3) and 15(2) above (and, so far as relating to those provisions, section 5(5) and 15(3) above) shall apply to any person who by virtue of this section fails to be treated as a servant of the government department in question; and

    (b)   section 6(6) above and paragraph 12 of Schedule 4 to this Act shall apply to a person in the public service of the Crown as they apply to any other person.

(3)   For the purposes of this Act—

    (a)   the constables under the direction and control of a chief officer of police shall be treated as his servants; and

    (b)   the members of any body of constables maintained otherwise than by a police authority shall be treated as the servants—

        (i) of the authority or person by whom that body is maintained, and

        (ii) in the case of any members of such a body who are under the direction and control of a chief officer, of that officer.

(4)   (*Applies to Scotland.*)

(5)   In the application of subsection (3) above to Northern Ireland, for the reference to a chief officer of police there shall be substituted a reference to the Chief Constable of the Royal Ulster Constabulary and for the reference

to a police authority there shall be substituted a reference to the Police Authority for Northern Ireland.

39.   Data held, and services provided, outside the United Kingdom

(1)   Subject to the following provisions of this section, this Act does not apply to a data user in respect of data held, or to a person carrying on a computer bureau in respect of services provided, outside the United Kingdom.

(2)   For the purposes of subsection (1) above—
  (a)   data shall be treated as held where the data user exercises the control referred to in subsection (5)(b) of section 1 above in relation to the data; and
  (b)   services shall be treated as provided where the person carrying on the computer bureau does any of the things referred to in subsection (6)(a) or (b) of that section.

(3)   Where a person who is not resident in the United Kingdom—
  (a)   exercises the control mentioned in paragraph (a) of subsection (2) above; or
  (b)   does any of the things mentioned in paragraph (b) of that subsection,

through a servant or agent in the United Kingdom, this Act shall apply as if that control were exercised or, as the case may be, those things were done in the United Kingdom by the servant or agent acting on his own account and not on behalf of the person whose servant or agent he is.

(4)   Where by virtue of subsection (3) above a servant or agent is treated as a data user or as a person carrying on a computer bureau he may be described for the purposes of registration by the position or office which he holds; and any such description in an entry in the register shall be treated as applying to the person for the time being holding the position or office in question.

(5)   This Act does not apply to data processed wholly outside the United Kingdom unless the data are used or intended to be used in the United Kingdom.

(6)   Sections 4(3)(e) and 5(2)(e) and subsection 12 above do not apply to the transfer of data which are already outside the United Kingdom; but references in the said section 12 to a contravention of the data protection principles include references to anything that would constitute such con-

travention if it occurred in relation to the data when held in the United Kingdom.

40.   Regulations, rules and orders

(1)   Any power conferred by this Act to make regulations, rules or orders shall be exercisable by statutory instrument.

(2)   Without prejudice to section 2(6) and 29(3) above, regulations, rules or orders under this Act may make different provision for different cases or circumstances.

(3)   Before making an order under any of the foregoing provisions of this Act the Secretary of State shall consult the Registrar.

(4)   No order shall be made under section 2(3), 4(8), 29, 30 or 34(2) above unless a draft of the order has been laid before and approved by a resolution of each House of Parliament.

(5)   A statutory instrument containing an order under section 21(9) or 37 above or rules under paragraph 4 of Schedule 3 to this Act shall be subject to annulment in pursuance of a resolution of either House of Parliament.

(6)   Regulations prescribing fees for the purposes of any provision of this Act or the period mentioned in section 8(2) above shall be laid before parliament after being made.

(7)   Regulations prescribing fees payable to the Registrar under this Act or the period mentioned in section 8(2) above shall be made after consultation with the Registrar and with the approval of the Treasury: and in making any such regulations the Secretary of State shall have regard to the desirability of securing that those fees are sufficient to offset the expenses incurred by the Registrar and the Tribunal in discharging their functions under this Act and any expenses of the Secretary of State in respect of the Tribunal.

41.   General interpretation

In addition to the provisions of sections 1 and 2 above, the following provisions shall have effect for the interpretation of this Act—

'business' includes any trade or profession;
'data equipment' means equipment for the automatic processing of data or for recording information so that it can be automatically processed;

'data material' means any document or other material used in connection
with data equipment;

'a de-registration notice' means a notice under section 11 above;

'enactment' includes an enactment passed after this Act;

'an enforcement notice' means a notice under section 10 above;

'the European Convention' means the Convention for the Protection of
Individuals with regard to Automatic Processing of Personal Data
which was opened for signature on 28th January 1981;

'government department' includes a Northern Ireland department and
any body or authority exercising statutory functions on behalf of
the Crown;

'prescribed' means prescribed by regulations made by the Secretary of
State;

'the Registrar' means the Data Protection Registrar;

'the register', except where the reference is to the register of companies,
means the register maintained under section 4 above and (except
where the reference is to a registered company, to the registered
office of a company or to registered post) references to registration
shall be construed accordingly;

'registered company' means a company registered under the enactments
relating to companies for the time being in force in any part of the
United Kingdom;

'a transfer prohibition notice' means a notice under section 12 above;

'the Tribunal' means the Data Protection Tribunal.

42.   Commencement and transitional provisions

(1)   No application for registration shall be made until such day as the
Secretary of State may by order appoint, and sections 5 and 15 above shall
not apply until the end of the period of six months beginning with the day.

(2)   Until the end of the period of two years beginning with the day
appointed under subsection (1) above the Registrar shall not have power—

(a) to refuse an application made in accordance with section 6 above
except on the ground mentioned in section 7(2)(a) above; or

(b) to serve an enforcement notice imposing requirements to be complied with, a de-registration notice expiring, or a transfer prohibition
notice imposing a prohibition taking effect, before the end of that
period.

(3)   Where the Registrar proposes to serve any person with an enforcement notice before the end of the period mentioned in subsection (2) above he shall, in determining the time by which the requirements of the notice are to be complied with, have regard to the probable cost of that person of complying with those requirements.

(4)   Section 21 above and paragraph l(b) of Schedule 4 to this Act shall not apply until the end of the period mentioned in subsection (2) above.

(5)   Section 22 above shall not apply to damage suffered before the end of the period mentioned in subsection (1) above and in deciding whether to refuse an application or serve a notice under Part II of this Act the Registrar shall treat the provision about accuracy in the fifth data protection principle as inapplicable until the end of that period and as inapplicable thereafter to data shown to have been held by the data user in question since before the end of that period.

(6)   Section 23 and 24(3) above shall not apply to damage suffered before the end of the period of two months beginning with the date on which this Act is passed.

(7)   Section 24(1) and (2) above shall not apply before the end of the period mentioned in subsection (1) above.

43.   Short title and extent

(1)   This Act may be cited as the Data Protection Act 1984.

(2)   This Act extends to Northern Ireland.

(3)   Her Majesty may by Order in Council direct that this Act shall extend to any of the Channel Islands with such exceptions and modifications as may be specified in the Order.

SCHEDULES

SCHEDULE 1

THE DATA PROTECTION PRINCIPLES

PART I

THE PRINCIPLES

Personal data held by data users

1.   The information to be contained in personal data shall be obtained, and personal data shall be processed, fairly and lawfully.

2.   Personal data shall be held only for one or more specified and lawful purposes.

3.   Personal data held for any purpose or purposes shall not be used or disclosed in any manner incompatible with that purpose or those purposes.

4.   Personal data held for any purpose or purposes shall be adequate, relevant and not excessive in relation to that purpose or those purposes.

5.   Personal data shall be accurate and, where necessary, kept up to date.

6.   Personal data held for any purpose or purposes shall not be kept for longer than is necessary for that purpose or those purposes.

7.   An individual shall be entitled—
     (a) at reasonable intervals and without undue delay or expense—
          (i) to be informed by any data user whether he holds personal data of which that individual is the subject; and
          (ii) to access to any such data held by a data user; and
     (b) where appropriate, to have such data corrected or erased.

Personal data held by data users or in respect of which services are provided by persons carrying on computer bureaux

8. Appropriate security measures shall be taken against unauthorized access to, or alteration, disclosure or destruction of, personal data and against accidental loss or destruction of personal data.

PART II

INTERPRETATION

The first principle

1.—(1) Subject to sub-paragraph (2) below, in determining whether information was obtained fairly regard shall be had to the method by which it was obtained, including in particular whether any person from whom it was obtained was deceived or misled as to the purpose or purposes for which it is to be held, used or disclosed.

(2) Information shall in any event be treated as obtained fairly if it is obtained from a person who—
   (a) is authorized by or under any enactment to supply it; or
   (b) is required to supply it by or under any enactment or by any convention or other instrument imposing an international obligation on the United Kingdom;

and in determining whether information was obtained fairly there shall be disregarded any disclosure of the information which is authorized or required by or under any enactment or required by any such convention or other instrument as aforesaid.

The second principle

2. Personal data shall not be treated as held for a specified purpose unless that purpose is described in particulars registered under this Act in relation to the data.

The third principle

3.   Personal data shall not be treated as used or disclosed in contravention of this principle unless—
   (a) used otherwise than for a purpose of a description registered under this Act in relation to the data; or
   (b) disclosed otherwise than to a person of a description so registered.

The fifth principle

4.   Any question whether or not personal data are accurate shall be determined as for the purposes of section 22 of this Act but, in the case of such data as are mentioned in subsection (2) of that section, this principle shall not be regarded as having been contravened by reason of any inaccuracy in the information there mentioned if the requirements specified in that subsection have been complied with.

The seventh principle

5.—(1) Paragraph (a) of this principle shall not be construed as conferring any rights inconsistent with section 21 of this Act.

(2)   In determining whether access to personal data is sought at reasonable intervals regard shall be had to the nature of the data, the purpose for which the data are held and the frequency with which the data are altered.

(3)   The correction or erasure of personal data is appropriate only where necessary for ensuring compliance with the other data protection principles.

The eighth principle

6.   Regard shall be had—
   (a) to the nature of the personal data and the harm that would result from such access, alteration, disclosure, loss or destruction as are mentioned in this principle; and
   (b) to the place where the personal data are stored, to security measures programmed into the relevant equipment and to measures taken for ensuring the reliability of staff having access to the data.

Use for historical, statistical or research purposes

7.   Where personal data are held for historical, statistical or research purposes and not used in such a way that damage or distress is, or is likely to be,
caused to any data subject—

   (a)   the information contained in the data shall not be regarded for the
         purposes of the first principle as obtained unfairly by reason only
         that its use for any such purpose was not disclosed when it was
         obtained; and

   (b)   the data may, notwithstanding the sixth principle, be kept indefi-
         nitely.

APPENDIX 5: THE LOCAL GOVERNMENT (ACCESS TO INFORMATION) ACT, 1985

An Act to provide for greater public access to local authority meetings, reports and documents subject to specified confidentiality provisions; to give local authorities duties to publish certain information; and for related purposes [16 July 1985]

1. Access to meetings and documents of certain authorities, committees and sub-committees

(1) After section 100 of the Local Government Act 1972 there shall be inserted the following—
'PART VA

ACCESS TO MEETINGS AND DOCUMENTS OF CERTAIN AUTHORITIES, COMMITTEES AND SUB-COMMITTEES

100A Admission to meetings of principal councils

(1) A meeting of a principal council shall be open to the public except to the extent that they are excluded (whether during the whole or part of the proceedings) under subsection (2) below or by resolution under subsection (4) below.

(2) The public shall be excluded from a meeting of a principal council during an item of business whenever it is likely, in view of the nature of the business to be transacted or the nature of the proceeding, that, if members of the public were present during that item, confidential infor-

mation would be disclosed to them in breach of the obligation of confidence; and nothing in this Part shall be taken to authorize or require the disclosure of confidential information in breach of the obligation of confidence.

(3) For the purpose of subsection (2) above, 'confidential information' means—

> (a) information furnished to the council by a Government department upon terms (however expressed) which forbid the disclosure of the information to the public; and
>
> (b) information the disclosure of which to the public is prohibited by or under any enactment or by the order of a court;

and, in either case, the reference to the obligation of confidence is to be construed accordingly.

(4) A principal council may by resolution exclude the public from a meeting during an item of business whenever it is likely, in view of the nature of the business to be transacted or the nature of the proceedings, that if members of the public were present during that item there would be disclosure to them of exempt information, as defined in section 100I below.

(5) A resolution under subsection (4) above shall—

> (a) identify the proceedings, or the part of the proceedings, to which it applies, and
>
> (b) state the description, in terms of Schedule 12A to this Act, of the exempt information giving rise to the exclusion of the public,

and where such a resolution is passed this section does not require the meeting to be open to the public during proceedings to which the resolution applies.

(6) The following provisions shall apply in relation to a meeting of a principal council, that is to say—

> (a) public notice of the time and place of the meeting shall be given by posting it at the offices of the council three clear days at least before the meeting or, if the meeting is convened at shorter notice, then at the time it is convened;
>
> (b) while the meeting is open to the public, the council shall not have power to exclude members of the public from the meeting; and
>
> (c) while the meeting is open to the public, duly accredited representatives of newspapers attending the meeting for the purpose of reporting the proceedings for those newspapers shall, so far as practicable, be afforded reasonable facilities for taking their report

and, unless the meeting is held in premises not belonging to the council or not on the telephone, for telephoning the report at their own expense.

(7)   Nothing in this section shall require a principal council to permit the taking of photographs of any proceedings, or the use of any means to enable persons not present to see or hear any proceedings (whether at the time or later), or the making of any oral report on any proceedings as they take place.

(8)   This section is without prejudice to any power of exclusion to suppress or prevent disorderly conduct or other misbehaviour at a meeting.

100B   Access to agenda and connected reports

(1)   Copies of the agenda for a meeting of a principal council and, subject to subsection (2) below, copies of any report for the meeting shall be open to inspection by members of the public at the offices of the council in accordance with subsection (3) below.

(2)   If the proper officer thinks fit, there may be excluded from the copies of reports provided in pursuance of subsection (1) above the whole of any report which, or any part which, relates only to items during which, in his opinion, the meeting is likely not to be open to the public.

(3)   Any document which is required by subsection (1) above to be open to inspection shall be so open at least three days before the meeting, except that—

(a)   where the meeting is convened at shorter notice, the copies of the agenda and reports shall be open to inspection from the time the meeting is convened, and

(b)   where an item is added to an agenda copies of which are open to inspection by the public, copies of the item (or of the revised agenda), and the copies of any report for the meeting relating to the item, shall be open to inspection from the time the item is added to the agenda;

but nothing in this subsection requires copies of any agenda, item or report to be open to inspection by the public until copies are available to members of the council.

(4)   An item of business may not be considered at a meeting of a principal council unless either—

(a) a copy of the agenda including the item (or a copy of the item) is open to inspection by members of the public in pursuance of subsection (1) above for at least three clear days before the meeting or, where the meeting is convened at shorter notice, from the time the meeting is convened; or

(b) by reason of special circumstances, which shall be specified in the minutes, the chairman of the meeting is of the opinion that the item should be considered at the meeting as a matter of urgency.

(5)   Where by virtue of subsection (2) above the whole or any part of a report for a meeting is not open to inspection by the public under subsection (1) above—

(a) every copy of the report or of the part shall be marked 'Not for publication'; and

(b) there shall be stated on every copy of the whole or any part of the report the description, in terms of Schedule 12A to this Act, of the exempt information by virtue of which the council are likely to exclude the public during the item to which the report relates.

(6)   Where a meeting of a principal council is required by section 100A above to be open to the public during the proceedings or any part of them, there shall be made available for the use of members of the public present at the meeting a reasonable number of copies of the agenda and, subject to subsection (8) below, of the reports for the meeting.

(7)   There shall, on request and on payment of postage or other necessary charge for transmission, be supplied for the benefit of any newspaper—

(a) a copy of the agenda for a meeting of a principal council and, subject to subsection (8) below, a copy of each of the reports for the meeting;

(b) such further statements or particulars, if any, as are necessary to indicate the nature of the items included in the agenda; and

(c) if the proper officer thinks fit in the case of any item, copies of any other documents supplied to members of the council in connection with the item.

(8)   Subsection (2) above applies in relation to copies of reports provided in pursuance of subsection (6) or (7) above as it applies in relation to copies of reports provided in pursuance of subsection (1) above.

100C   Inspection of minutes and other documents after meetings

(1)   After a meeting of a principal council the following documents shall be open to inspection by members of the public at the offices of the council until the expiration of the period of six years beginning with the date of the meeting, namely—

- (a) the minutes, or a copy of the minutes, of the meeting, excluding so much of the minutes of proceedings during which the meeting was not open to the public as discloses exempt information;
- (b) where applicable, a summary under subsection (2) below;
- (c) a copy of the agenda for the meeting; and
- (d) a copy of so much of any report for the meeting as relates to any item during which the meeting was open to the public.

(2)   Where, in consequence of the exclusion of parts of the minutes which disclose exempt information, the document open to inspection under subsection (1)(a) above does not provide members of the public with a reasonably fair and coherent record of the whole or part of the proceedings, the proper officer shall make a written summary of the proceedings or the part, as the case may be, which provides such a record without disclosing the exempt information.

100D   Inspection of background papers

(1)   Subject, in the case of section 100C(1), to subsection (2) below, if and so long as copies of the whole or part of a report for a meeting of a principal council are required by section 100B (1) or 100C(1) above to be open to inspection by members of the public—

- (a) copies of a list, compiled by the proper officer, of the background papers for the report or the part of the report, and
- (b) at least one copy of each of the documents included in that list,

shall also be open to their inspection at the offices of the council.

(2)   Subsection (1) above does not require a copy of the list, or of any document included in the list, to be open to inspection after the expiration of the period of four years beginning with the date of the meeting.

(3)   Where a copy of any of the background papers for a report is required by subsection (1) above to be open to inspection by members of the public, the copy shall be taken for the purposes of this Part to be so open if arrangements exist for its production to members of the public as soon as is reasonably practicable after the making of a request to inspect the copy.

(4)   Nothing in this section—
   (a)   requires any document which discloses exempt information to be included in the list referred to in subsection (1) above; or
   (b)   without prejudice to the generality of subsection (2) of section 100A above, requires or authorizes the inclusion in the list of any document which, if open to inspection by the public, would disclose confidential information in breach of the obligation of confidence, within the meaning of that subsection.

(5)   For the purposes of this section the background papers for a report are those documents relating to the subject matter of the report which—
   (a)   disclose any facts or matters on which, in the opinion of the proper officer, the report or an important part of the report is based, and
   (b)   have, in his opinion, been relied on to a material extent in preparing the report,

but do not include any published works.

100E   Application to committees and sub-committees

(1)   Sections 100A to 100D above shall apply in relation to a committee or sub-committee of a principal council as they apply in relation to a principal council.

(2)   In the application by virtue of this section of sections 100A to 100D above in relation to a committee or sub-committee
   (a)   section 100A(6)(a) shall be taken to have been complied with if the notice is given by posting it at the time there mentioned at the offices of every constituent principal council and, if the meeting of the committee or sub-committee to which that section so applies is to be held at premises other than the offices of such a council, at those premises;
   (b)   for the purposes of section 100A(6)(c), premises belonging to a constituent principal council shall be treated as belonging to the committee or sub-committee; and
   (c)   for the purposes of sections 100B(1), 100C(1) and 100(D)(1), offices of any constituent principal council shall be treated as offices of the committee or sub-committee.

(3)   Any reference in this Part to a committee or sub-committee of a principal council is a reference to—

(a) a committee which is constituted under an enactment specified in section 101(9) below or which is appointed by one or more principal councils under section 102 below; or

(b) a joint committee not falling within paragraph (a) above which is appointed or established under any enactment by two or more principal councils and is not a body corporate; or

(c) a sub-committee appointed or established under any enactment by one or more committees falling within paragraph (a) or (b) above.

(4)   Any reference in this Part to a constituent principal council, in relation to a committee or sub-committee, is a reference—

(a) in the case of a committee, to the principal council, or any of the principal councils, of which it is a committee; and

(b) in the case of a sub-committee, to any principal council which, by virtue of paragraph (a) above, is a constituent principal council in relation to the committee, or any of the committees, which established or appointed the sub-committee.

100F   Additional rights of access to documents for members of principal councils

(1)   Any document which is in the possession or under the control of a principal council and contains material relating to any business to be transacted at a meeting of the council or a committee or sub-committee of the council shall, subject to subsection (2) below, be open to inspection by any member of the council.

(2)   Where it appears to the proper officer that a document discloses exempt information of a description for the time being falling within any of paragraphs 1 to 6, 9, 11, 12 and 14 of Part 1 of Schedule 12A to this Act, subsection (1) above does not require the document to be open to inspection.

(3)   The Secretary of State may by order amend subsection (2) above—

(a) by adding to the descriptions of exempt information to which that subsection refers for the time being; or

(b) by removing any description of exempt information to which it refers for the time being.

(4)   Any statutory instrument containing an order under subsection (3) above shall be subject to annulment in pursuance of a resolution of either House of Parliament.

(5)   The rights conferred by this section on a member of a principal council are in addition to any other rights he may have apart from this section.

100G   Principal councils to publish additional information

(1)   A principal council shall maintain a register stating—
  (a)   the name and address of every member of the council for the time being and the ward or division which he represents; and
  (b)   the name and address of every member of each committee or sub-committee of the council for the time being.

(2)   A principal council shall maintain a list—
  (a)   specifying those powers of the council which, for the time being, are exercisable from time to time by officers of the council in pursuance of arrangements made under this Act or any other enactment for their discharge by those officers; and
  (b)   stating the title of the officer by whom each of the powers so specified is for the time being so exercisable;

but this subsection does not require a power to be specified in the list if the arrangements for its discharge by the officer are made for a specified period not exceeding six months.

(3)   There shall be kept at the offices of every principal council a written summary of the rights—
  (a)   to attend meetings of a principal council and of committees and sub-committees of a principal council, and
  (b)   to inspect and copy documents and to be furnished with documents,

which are for the time being conferred by this Part, Part XI below and such other enactments as the Secretary of State by order specifies.

(4)   The register maintained under subsection (1) above, the list maintained under subsection (2) above and the summary kept under subsection (3) above shall be open to inspection by the public at the offices of the council.

100H   Supplemental provisions and offences

(1)   A document directed by any provision of this Part to be open to inspection shall be so open at all reasonable hours and—
  (a)   in the case of a document open to inspection by virtue of section 100D(1) above, upon payment of such reasonable fee as may be required for the facility; and

(b) in any other case, without payment.

(2)   Where a document is open to inspection by a person under any provision of this Part, the person may, subject to subsection (3) below—

(a) make copies of or extracts from the document, or

(b) require the person having custody of the document to supply to him a photographic copy of or of extracts from the document, upon payment of such reasonable fee as may be required for the facility.

(3)   Subsection (2) above does not require or authorize the doing of any act which infringes the copyright in any work except that, where the owner of the copyright is a principal council, nothing done in pursuance of that subsection shall constitute an infringement of the copyright.

(4)   If, without reasonable excuse, a person having the custody of a document which is required by section 100B(1) or 100C(1) above to be open to inspection by the public—

(a) intentionally obstructs any person exercising a right conferred by this Part to inspect, or to make a copy of or extracts from the document, or

(b) refuses to furnish copies to any person entitled to obtain them under any provision of this Part,

he shall be liable on summary conviction to a fine not exceeding level 1 on the standard scale.

(5)   Where any accessible document for a meeting to which this subsection applies—

(a) is supplied to, or open to inspection by, a member of the public, or

(b) is supplied for the benefit of any newspaper, in pursuance of section 100B(7) above,

the publication thereby of any defamatory matter contained in the document shall be privileged unless the publication is proved to be made with malice.

(6)   Subsection (5) above applies to any meeting of a principal council and any meeting of a committee or sub-committee of a principal council; and, for the purposes of that subsection, the 'accessible documents' for a meeting are the following—

(a) any copy of the agenda or of any item included in the agenda for the meeting;

(b) any such further statements or particulars for the purpose of indicating the nature of any item included in the agenda as are mentioned in section 100B(7)(b) above;

(c) any copy of a document relating to such an item which is supplied
for the benefit of a newspaper in pursuance of section 100B(7)(c)
above;

(d) any copy of the whole or part of a report for the meeting;

(e) any copy of the whole or part of any background papers for a report
for the meeting, within the meaning of section 100D above.

(7) The rights conferred by this Part to inspect, copy and be furnished with
documents are in addition, and without prejudice, to any such rights conferred by or under any other enactment.

100I   Exempt information and power to vary Schedule 12A

(1) The descriptions of information which are, for the purposes of this Part,
exempt information are those for the time being specified in Part I of
Schedule 12A to this Act, but subject to any qualifications contained in Part
II of that Schedule; and Part III has effect for the interpretation of that
Schedule.

(2) The Secretary of State may by order vary Schedule 12A to this Act by
adding to it any description or other provision or by deleting from it or
varying any description or other provision for the time being specified or
contained in it.

(3) The Secretary of State may exercise the power conferred by subsection
(2) above by amending any Part of Schedule 12A to this Act, with or without
amendment of any other Part.

(4) Any statutory instrument containing an order under this section shall
be subject to annulment in pursuance of a resolution of either House of
Parliament.

100J   Application to new authorities, Common Council, etc.

(1) Except in this section, any reference in this Part to a principal council
includes a reference to—

(a) the Inner London Education Authority;

(b) a joint authority;

(c) the Common Council;

(d) a joint board or joint committee falling within subsection (2) below;

      (e) a combined police authority which is a body corporate;

      (f) a combined fire authority.

(2)   A joint board or joint committee falls within this subsection if—

      (a) it is constituted under any enactment as a body corporate; and

      (b) it discharges functions of two or more principal councils;

and for the purposes of this subsection any body falling within paragraph (a), (b) or (c) of subsection (1) above shall be treated as a principal council.

(3)   In its application by virtue of subsection (1) above in relation to a body falling within paragraph (a), (b), (d), (e) or (f) of that subsection, section 100A (6)(a) above shall have effect with the insertion after the word 'council' of the words '(and, if the meeting is to be held at premises other than those offices, at those premises)'.

(4)   In its application by virtue of subsection (1) above, section 100G(1)(a) above shall have effect—

      (a) in relation to a joint authority or a combined police authority, with the substitution for the words from 'ward' onwards of the words 'name or description of the body which appointed him'; and

      (b) in relation to a joint board or joint committee falling within subsection (2) above, with the omission of the words from 'and the ward' onwards; and

      (c) in relation to a combined fire authority, with the substitution for the words 'ward or division' of the words 'constituent area'.

(5)   In this section 'combined fire authority' means a fire authority constituted by a combination scheme under the Fire Services Act 1947.

100K   Interpretation and application of Part VA

(1)   In this Part—

    'committee or sub-committee of a principal council' shall be construed in accordance with section 100E(3) above;

    'constituent principal council' shall be construed in accordance with section 100E(4) above;

    'copy', in relation to any document, includes a copy made from a copy;

    'exempt information' has the meaning given by section 100I above;

    'information' includes an expression of opinion, any recommendations and any decision taken;

    'newspaper' includes—

(a) a news agency which systematically carries on the business of selling and supplying reports or information to news-papers; and

(b) any organization which is systematically engaged in collecting news—

(i) for sound or television broadcasts; or

(ii) for programmes to be included in a cable programme service which is or does not require to be licensed;
'principal council' shall be construed in accordance with section 100J above.

(2)   Any reference in this Part to a meeting is a reference to a meeting held after 1st April 1986'.

(2)   After Schedule 12 to the Local Government Act 1972 there shall be inserted, as Schedule 12A, the Schedule set out in Part I of Schedule I to this Act.

2.   (*Applies to Scotland only.*)

3.   **Consequential amendments and repeals**

(1)   The enactments mentioned in Schedule 2 to this Act shall have effect with the amendments there specified, being amendments consequential on the provisions of this Act.

(2)   The enactments mentioned in Schedule 3 to this Act are hereby repealed to the extent specified in the third column of that Schedule.

4.   **Extent**

Except for this section and section 3 so far as it relates to paragraph 3 of Schedule 2, this Act shall not extend to Northern Ireland.

5.   **Commencement**

This Act shall come into force on 1st April 1986.

6.   Short title

This Act may be cited as the Local Government (Access to Information) Act 1985.

SCHEDULES

SCHEDULE I

Sections 1 and 2

EXEMPT INFORMATION

PART I

SCHEDULE TO BE INSERTED INTO THE LOCAL GOVERNMENT ACT **1972**

SCHEDULE **12A**

ACCESS TO INFORMATION: EXEMPT INFORMATION

PART I

DESCRIPTIONS OF EXEMPT INFORMATION

1.   Information relating to a particular employee, former employee or applicant to become an employee of, or a particular office-holder, former office-holder or applicant to become an office-holder under, the authority.

2.   Information relating to a particular employee, former employee or applicant to become an employee of, or a particular officer, former officer or applicant to become an officer appointed by—

(a)   a magistrates' court committee, within the meaning of section 19 of the Justices of the Peace Act 1979; or

(b)   a probation committee appointed under paragraph 2 of Schedule 3 to the Powers of Criminal Courts Act 1973.

3.   Information relating to any particular occupier or former occupier of, or applicant for, accommodation provided by or at the expense of the authority.

4.   Information relating to any particular applicant for, or recipient or former recipient of, any service provided by the authority.

5.   Information relating to any particular applicant for, or recipient or former recipient of, any financial assistance provided by the authority.

6.   Information relating to the adoption, care, fostering or education of any particular child.

7.   Information relating to the financial or business affairs of any particular person (other than the authority).

8.   The amount of any expenditure proposed to be incurred by the authority under any particular contract for the acquisition of property or the supply of goods or services.

9.   Any terms proposed or to be proposed by or to the authority in the course of negotiations for a contract for the acquisition or disposal of property or the supply of goods or services.

10. The identity of the authority (as well as of any other person, by virtue of paragraph 7 above) as the person offering any particular tender for a contract for the supply of goods or services.

11. Information relating to any consultations or negotiations, or contemplated consultations or negotiations, in connection with any labour relations matter arising between the authority or a Minister of the Crown and employees of, or office-holders under, the authority.

12. Any instructions to counsel and any opinion of counsel (whether or not in connection with any proceedings) and any advice received, information obtained or action to be taken in connection with—
   (a) any legal proceedings by or against the authority, or
   (b) the determination of any matter affecting the authority,

(whether, in either case, proceedings have been commenced or are in contemplation).

13. Information which, if disclosed to the public, would reveal that the authority proposes—
   (a) to give under any enactment a notice under or by virtue of which requirements are imposed on a person; or

(b) to make an order or direction under any enactment.

14. Any action taken or to be taken in connection with the prevention, investigation or prosecution of crime.

15. The identity of a protected informant.

APPENDIX 6: HOW TO TRACE COMPANY INFORMATION

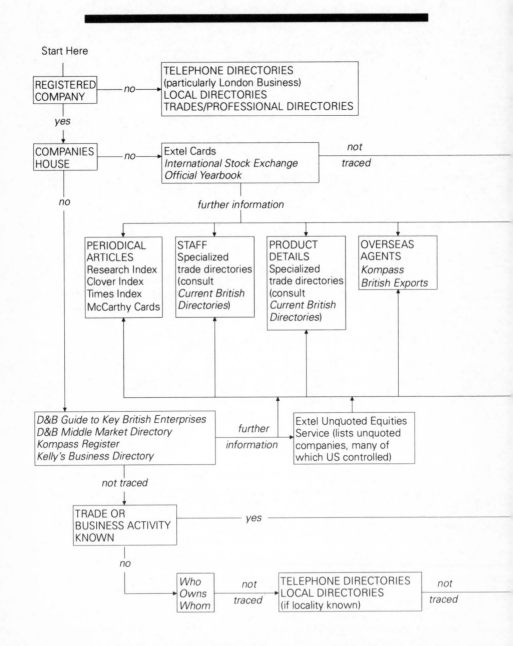

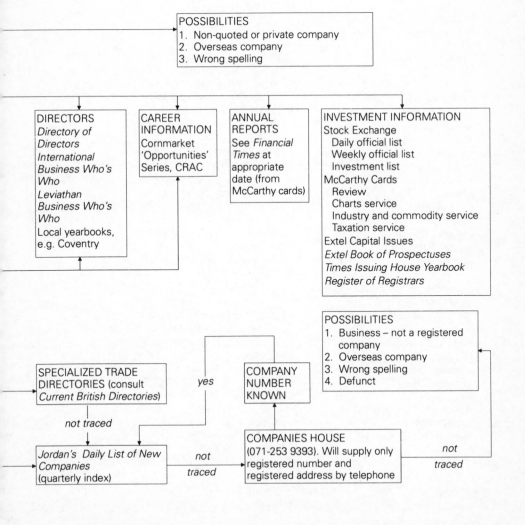

POSSIBILITIES
1. Non-quoted or private company
2. Overseas company
3. Wrong spelling

DIRECTORS
Directory of Directors
International Business Who's Who
Leviathan Business Who's Who
Local yearbooks, e.g. Coventry

CAREER INFORMATION
Cornmarket 'Opportunities' Series, CRAC

ANNUAL REPORTS
See *Financial Times* at appropriate date (from McCarthy cards)

INVESTMENT INFORMATION
Stock Exchange
  Daily official list
  Weekly official list
  Investment list
McCarthy Cards
  Review
  Charts service
  Industry and commodity service
  Taxation service
Extel Capital Issues
Extel Book of Prospectuses
Times Issuing House Yearbook
Register of Registrars

POSSIBILITIES
1. Business – not a registered company
2. Overseas company
3. Wrong spelling
4. Defunct

SPECIALIZED TRADE DIRECTORIES (consult *Current British Directories*)

yes

COMPANY NUMBER KNOWN

not traced

Jordan's Daily List of New Companies (quarterly index)

not traced

COMPANIES HOUSE (071-253 9393). Will supply only registered number and registered address by telephone

not traced

INDEX